Teen People

Celebrity

STYLE GUIDE

Celebrity STYLE

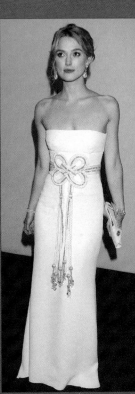

GUIDE

CONTENTS

EDITOR'S LETTER

Brrrrring! After the alarm clock blares and school or work beckons, you are inevitably faced with making your first big decision of the day: What am I going to wear? And what a decision it is. Because unless you are lucky enough to have that computerized clothes-matching thingie that *Clueless*'s Cher Horowitz has in her gi-normous walk-in closet, you are going to have to do some fast thinking. Breakfast, last-minute homework, and class await, as do your sure-to-be styling friends—and maybe even that certain someone whose eye you've been dying to catch.

If you're like most people, the what-to-wear decision is a daily battle with your closet—and your inner self. Does this skirt make me look hot . . . or not? Does this dress make me look like I'm trying too hard? And these jeans—they are the exact same ones that Jessica Simpson has, so why do they make me look more like Marge Simpson?

Well, guess what? Jessica Simpson deals with what-to-wear drama too . . . well, she does whenever her $3,000-a-day stylist has the day off! At *Teen People*, we're always dressing the hottest celebrities—along with real teens, just like you—so we know all about your style dilemmas. In the pages that follow, *Teen People*'s fashion team will show you how to build a wardrobe that is right for YOU and that will help you answer that daily "What am I going to wear?" question with confidence, ease—even excitement. This book is packed with practical, need-to-know fashion tips: from finding the perfect pair of jeans (size and shape of back pockets matter!) to the best bra for your body to how to put together a star-quality closet on your budget. We all have an inner fashionista, and finally, here is the perfect book to help you bring out yours! After all, your style is your story. So let's get started, shall we?!

—Lori Majewski
Managing Editor

1
in search of
TRUE

STYLE

FASHION, TRENDS, AND STYLE

Rachel Bilson is so confident in her style, she lets this dress make a statement on its own, without busy accessories.

WHILE FASHION AND TRENDS ARE CONSTANTLY CHANGING, ONE-OF-A-KIND STYLE CAN LAST FOREVER.

Style is a more essential part of our lives than most people think. On the pages of *Teen People,* on your favorite TV shows, projected on movie screens, on the Web, and at school, fashion and trends play a big part in how we see the world. Clothes give us clues about who people are and what they like, and provide us with an outlet to express ourselves every day. The way you dress telegraphs more about who you are than you realize. Think of it this way: Even before you've had a chance to crack a joke, introduce yourself, or say hello, people have made decisions about you based on the way you dress. Once you sort out your own distinct style, getting dressed every day (not to mention shopping) is bound to be a lot more satisfying and fun.

CONSIDER THIS:

- The clothes you choose to wear, and the ways you wear them, can identify the music, hobbies, or interests you like and tell the world whether you're outgoing, girly, rebellious, quirky—you name it.

- When an actor plays a role, the wardrobe department helps define the character by dressing the actor in a particular style. Whether you realize it or not, you're doing the same thing at home in front of the mirror every morning when you get dressed.

- If you throw on that same old T-shirt and jeans without giving it much thought (or worse, just because hundreds of other people you know are wearing the same exact thing) you may be passing up an opportunity to show YOUR best, most interesting side to the world.

STYLE GODDESSES: WERE THEY BORN THAT WAY?

Some lucky people are just born with great style, great taste, and a great sense of color. But the truth is, most of us aren't. It's hard to imagine that someone like Jessica Simpson or Mandy Moore has ever second-guessed her style, but trust us, it happens… all the time.

They're not created equal

WHY BEING A CELEBRITY ISN'T AS FUN AS IT SEEMS SOMETIMES

Celebrities admit to *Teen People* that they aren't always happy with their bodies and have a hard time finding clothes that make them feel confident. Imagine leaving the house every day knowing that your picture will probably be taken and your outfit criticized by millions of people. Talk about pressure! Before a team of fashion stylists worked them over, many celebrities had the same concerns about clothes (and made the same mistakes) as the rest of us.

HOW WE CAN HELP!

After interviewing, photographing, dressing, and obsessing over the fashion icons of the moment, the editors of *Teen People* have learned a few things about how to wear clothes and how to teach our readers to dress their best.

Here's the good news: You don't have to get in on every trend, or even be that interested in fashion, to have an individual style. But you do have to know what you like, what looks good on you, and how to build a solid and fun wardrobe that will help you feel pulled together and confident without spending a fortune. When you get this down, it's easy to show the world the most amazing version of you every single day.

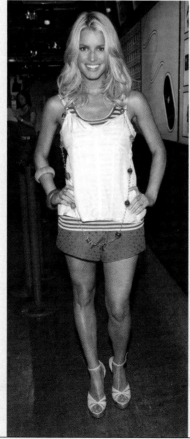

Jessica Simpson's outfit shows off her eye for fun trends (shorts with heels, bangles, long beads).

In this sleek tube dress, **Mischa Barton** shows off her long limbs and her sophisticated side.

KNOW THE DIFFERENCE BETWEEN FASHION, TRENDS, AND STYLE

ALL YOU NEED TO KNOW ABOUT…FASHION

- Fashion is what the people who make clothes—especially expensive clothes—think everyone should wear from season to season.

- Fashion is constantly changing. One season, designers will say that black is chic and color isn't. The next season, black is suddenly boring and white is in, or purple, or lime green, or whatever. One season, it's all about stripes. The next, stripes are dull and flowers are cool. Short skirts are in one year; the next season long skirts are the must-have.

- That said, we need creative designers to show us new ideas that we may never think of on our own. Look at Gwen Stefani and all of the inventive looks she comes up with every season. There are hundreds and hundreds of designers around the world working to create new concepts to love. But in the everyday life of the average teenager, fashion usually takes a backseat to trends.

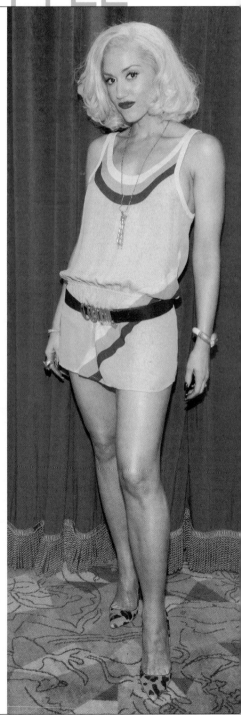

Hey, big trender! **Paris Hilton** has never met a fashion fad she didn't like.

ALL YOU NEED TO KNOW ABOUT...TRENDS

- The latest, of-the-minute items, like long, dangly jewelry that everyone has to have, is a trend. It's something you see people wearing—on the street, at school, or at the mall—that's suddenly everywhere and then disappears just as quickly.

- Trucker hats are trendy. Jeans that are so shredded they look like they're hanging by a single thread are trendy. Gigantic pink sunglasses that cover your whole face are trendy. (Even little dogs are trendy.) Leg warmers are trendy.

- Trends can be revisited, until someone realizes that it's kind of silly and everyone gets over it. All it takes is one "cool" person to be photographed wearing an "old" trend, like leg warmers, and, *bam!* Leg warmers are "in" again. The person who can wear leg warmers and spark an international trend has style, which leads us to the next point.

ALL YOU NEED TO KNOW ABOUT... STYLE

- True style is unique personal expression. It's applying your imagination to the clothes you wear and how you live. It's a way of dressing to match your character that no one else can imitate.

- **Cameron Diaz** has her own style—whether she's wearing casual jeans or haute couture.

- Once you discover your own style, fashion and trends become a lot less important. They're great for giving you ideas but won't dictate how you dress.

- It's easier to make sense of stores when you know exactly what you like and precisely what looks great on you, right? While there are no absolute rules about style, there are a few guidelines: It's rarely sloppy (no exposed undies or pj's at school) or stolen (copying your best friend's every move is the opposite of style), and it's always occasion-appropriate (no jeans to the prom).

- Your style will also change as your tastes change, so don't be afraid of experimenting a little. But the things that make you *you* will be a constant, and staying true to yourself will help you weed out the trends and fashions that won't work for you and find those that will.

WHAT'S YOUR STYLE?

While you don't have to settle on a single look, it's important to understand your own taste and dress in a way that reflects who you are on the inside. Style is all about sorting out your likes and dislikes and presenting the best version of you to the world. Here's how.

Emmy Rossum

Joss Stone

Sarah Jessica Parker

Kirsten Dunst

1. TAKE A LONG, HARD LOOK AT YOUR CLOSET:

What do you see? Put together these clues from your wardrobe to help solve your style mystery. Odds are, you'll find you're a combination of styles.

- Do you have a lot of skirts? If they're full or pleated, your style might be ladylike or kind of preppy (think Emmy Rossum or **Anne Hathaway**). If they're long and hippie-ish, you may be a little bohemian (like Joss Stone).

- Do you have a lot of ruffles and floral prints? That means you may favor feminine, flirty clothes. (Like Sarah Jessica Parker does.)

- Are you mostly a jeans or pants person? You may have a laid-back California style (like **Jennifer Aniston**).

- A little bit of everything in your closet? You're more of a free spirit, and Kirsten Dunst or **Lindsay Lohan** may be your style twin.

TIP: You can take style cues from your favorite stars and still have a look that's all yours. No one is suggesting you become a clone, but there's nothing wrong with borrowing a good idea from time to time and making it your own.

2. THINK OF YOUR FAVORITE OUTFITS.

You may need to look through a few photo albums for this section. Scan your snapshots, then focus on your favorites. What do these pictures tell you?

* Do you love the outfit you're wearing?
* What color is it?
* What's the cut and style?
* Does it make you feel good about the way your body looks?
* Does it flatter the features you like most and draw less attention to the ones you're still working on?

Take note of all of the details—the earrings you were wearing, a necklace, the jacket. These are the colors, shapes, and styles that make you look and feel your best, so shop for similarly flattering things.

3. WHAT WERE YOU WEARING THE LAST TIME SOMEONE PAID YOU A BIG COMPLIMENT?

If someone tells you that you look great in what you're wearing, you probably feel great in it, too. Remember your favorite outfits next time you're out shopping, and look for anything that reminds you of them, whether it's a similar color, cut, or attitude.

4. WHEN YOU SHOP, WHAT IS YOUR EYE DRAWN TO?

Next time you're "just browsing" at your favorite store, pay attention to where your eyes wander. What fabrics do you reach out to touch and feel? If you can't tear your eyes away from crisp cotton shirts, maybe you love classic looks. If you're always trying on big, slouchy, cowl-necked or off-the-shoulder tops, you've got a more bohemian edge. Do you love ripped jeans? You've got a little rebel inside of you. If you like velvet more than corduroy, you're more glamorous than sporty. If you can't resist an outrageous pattern or out-there outfit, and couldn't be bothered with a plain old T-shirt, you're a true original.

5. WHOSE STYLE DO YOU ADMIRE THE MOST?

Here's where all of those hours you spend flipping through your favorite magazines really pay off. Think of your favorite celebrity photos. What is it about their style that you're drawn to? Do you love **Rachel Bilson's** knack for combining vintage clothes with new things? If you do, then why not try shopping at a second-hand store? Do you love how Ciara always tucks her pants into boots? Give it a shot. If you can identify your favorite style when you see it, you're one step closer to making it your own.

Ciara

6. KEEP A FASHION SCRAPBOOK

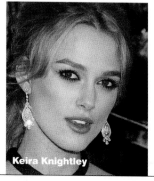

Keira Knightley

Rip out the pictures you love from magazines or catalogs (or print out copies of your favorite online shots), then paste them into a notebook. Once the pages start filling up, you might start noticing a theme. If dangly earrings keep showing up, you may be having a Keira Knightley or **Mandy Moore** moment. If ladylike looks from the red carpet are in there over and over again, try ditching your jeans every once in a while in favor of a skirt. As the pictures pile up, you'll be able to keep track of how your taste is changing and see what is just a passing, trendy fad, and what, months later, is your true style.

TEEN PEOPLE'S
ALL-TIME FAVORITE STYLE ICONS

It was a tough call, but we were able to single out ten stars who have an easy-to-identify look, each star representing a different way to fit in with fashion and stand out in a crowd. Whether spotted on the street with a shopping bag or posing on the red carpet, these stars always look comfortable and confident.

LINDSAY LOHAN *Free Spirit*

She's gone from cute little girl to curvy redhead to svelte blonde to serious brunette, and her clothes have changed as much as she has. In *Mean Girls*, she transformed herself on screen from fresh-scrubbed to "plastic" with a few key wardrobe changes. She's made a similar transition in real life.

Lindsay loves to use clothes to call attention to herself, but when she settles down and puts on a demure designer dress, she looks terrific. This is a sign of someone who clearly loves clothes, and clothes love her right back.

HER LOOK:

- She's seen shopping everywhere, usually carrying to-die-for handbags and wearing cowboy boots.
- It's her sassy side—in tiny minidresses with halter or keyhole necklines—that people seem to love.
- When the occasion calls for it, Lindsay is confident enough to put on an elegant dress and keep her look subtle and (relatively) low-key.

JESSICA SIMPSON *Feminine and Flirty*

Texans like Jessica are famous for doing things in a big, bold way. And for her, it's that extra helping of girly glamour that defines her style.

Jessica's icon status didn't happen overnight. In 1999, she wore simple tank tops and straight hair for photo shoots. Not anymore. These days, there isn't a designer around who doesn't want her to wear his or her clothes, and the more they show off her curvy body, the better.

HER LOOK:

- She likes bold prints and patterns, and for big nights on the town, she prefers skirts and dresses to pants.

- If she wears black, it's almost always short and sassy. She likes her earrings big and dangly and her heels high.

- In a T-shirt worn with a chunky belt and jeans tucked into cowboy boots or a floor-grazing gown, she looks cool, confident, and very much like the girly-girl she is.

BEYONCÉ *High Glamour*

Beyoncé Knowles has a big presence, and she needs clothes with lots of personality to match. Beaded gowns and bold patterns complement her caramel-colored skin and deep golden hair. Even in the early days of Destiny's Child, she loved sequins, beads, and bikini tops, and would take advantage of as many wardrobe changes as she could handle. It's hard to imagine her ever being low-key. Her nonstop glamour and high-wattage smile make it hard for anyone to take their eyes off of her.

HER LOOK:
• Even off-stage, Beyoncé will never be spotted without a few prominent accessories of some kind: gigantic gold earrings, a beautiful leather belt, and cuff bracelets; a sarong and a belly chain to go over her bikini; or maybe a hat.

• Sure, she'll wear denim, either as a curve-flattering skirt or jeans with a sexy, silky top and heels.

• For Beyoncé, bigger is definitely better, from an oversized designer handbag to shoulder-grazing chandelier earrings to her hair styles.

JENNIFER ANISTON *Malibu Cool*

Snapped on the run in an airport or on a movie set, Jennifer Aniston is one of those women who wear clothes well. For the red carpet, she chooses understated jewelry; very little makeup; loose, slightly wavy or poker-straight hair; and solid-color shift dresses that look both comfortable and elegant. As a result, she looks effortlessly radiant. She does well on her days off, too—in a T-shirt and jeans or a bikini top and drawstring pants, she never looks undone, just relaxed and confident. Jennifer may be most famous for her hairstyles (and her ex-husband), but we think she deserves props for her laid-back fashion sense, too.

HER LOOK:

- In a simple dress and sandals or in crisp white pants and aviator glasses, she has a way of appearing totally chic.
- Her secret? Wearing clothes that fit her lean, athletic frame perfectly.
- She avoids obvious trends and overloading on accessories. And she knows her own style so well that you'll never catch her in a busy print or pattern that would ruin the clean lines she loves.

GWEN STEFANI *True Original*

How do you even begin to talk about Gwen Stefani's style? It's hard not to be overshadowed by four fashion-obsessed Japanese dancers when you're performing onstage, but Gwen, who draws inspiration from the young, hyper-stylish girls in Tokyo's Harajuku district, could never be outshined. Her platinum hair and permanently red lips are the only things about this Orange County girl's style that don't change much. Never content to look like anyone else, Gwen's now designing her own line of clothes and shoes, L.A.M.B., which is just as outrageous as she is. She has confessed to having a "fatal attraction to cuteness," and it's obvious. She refuses to grow up completely, and that's reflected in her fun and fabulous style.

HER LOOK:

- She has worn everything from her signature bikini tops, track pants, and sneakers in clashing colors and patterns to camouflage shorts and over-the-knee boots. When she's spotted on the street, she still likes sporty basics like bomber jackets, baseball caps, and cargo pants.

- For evening and on the red carpet, she likes to wear glamorous 1940s-inspired cocktail dresses and corset tops.

- Somehow, through all of these phases and fads, she still manages to maintain more or less the same combination of styles: slightly sporty, over-the-top, really glamorous, and totally original.

KIRSTEN DUNST
Downtown Eccentric

No matter if she's wearing a denim miniskirt and Converse sneakers or a Chanel dress and heels, Kirsten Dunst has a casual, cool-girl style that's difficult to imitate but easy to understand. Here's the thing: She never looks like she's trying very hard. Even at the Oscars, when she throws on a black lace dress and bright-red lipstick (no baseball-sized diamonds for her)—and although she could have dressed in 15 minutes—she looks just right. Away from the red carpet, Kirsten prefers loose-fitting, flowy dresses and messy, slept-in hair, which adds to her slightly edgy appeal. Her wide smile says that she's having a little bit more fun than the typical, serious downtown girl, and likes being different from everyone else.

HER LOOK:

- Kirsten's style is proof that sometimes less *is* more. If you feel uncomfortable trying to be fashionable, sometimes the best option is to relax.

- She will choose chic-and-modest over drop-dead-sexy almost every time, which fits with her smart, independent image.

- With her hair pulled back and sandals on, she looks like a regular girl…never a celebrity who's trying to look like a regular girl! And that's why we love her.

EVE *Sexy and Strong*

Finding the balance between tough and pretty is always a challenge, but Eve Jeffers, who began her career as a rapper in Philadelphia, does it with flair. Maybe it's because she's managed to maintain her bad-girl edge even when she sits in the front row of a fashion show. Sure, she'll show up to an event in the occasional prim and proper dress, but you always get the feeling she's just minutes away from getting back in her skinny jeans and boots and slipping on a slinky tank top. In the *Barbershop* movies, she was able to hold her own as the only woman in a cast of men. On her UPN show, *Eve,* she plays a Miami-based fashion designer who loves sexy, shiny, colorful clothes. And her real-life persona is like a combination of those two characters.

HER LOOK:

• She looks great in big, slouchy tops over leggings, which always show both her feminine and her tomboy sides.

• Every once in a while, she'll play up her girly side for an event—and do it really well!

• In her downtime, you might catch her with a knit cap slightly askew, windshield-sized sunglasses, and lots of lip gloss—the perfect combination of the things she loves. And she'll always make it look fabulous in her own distinct way.

HILARY DUFF *Sweet-Natured Rebel*

It can't be easy to grow up on camera. As Lizzie McGuire, Hilary Duff had to buy a bra on national television! Well, it wasn't her bra—it was her character's—but it's still an experience that most teenagers (thankfully) will never have. As she's outgrown her character's pink T-shirts, Hilary's developed a new style of her own. She's both a movie star and a singer now, but, judging by the clothes she wears, she identifies more with the rock side of her resume. Morphing from teenage sweetie into stylish adult with the whole world watching is no mean feat—but Hilary Duff is managing beautifully.

HER LOOK:

- In skinny jeans and long tank tops, tall boots, extra-long beads, and long, uneven bangs, if she wasn't onstage, she'd fit in easily backstage, hanging out with her favorite bands.

- She has a flair for the dramatic: If her dress seems demure from the front, you can bet it's got a low-cut back!

- She's aware of proportion: She balances ruffles with slim shapes so as not to overwhelm her small frame.

NICOLE RICHIE *Designer Princess*

While Nicole Richie has always been surrounded by celebrities and expensive clothes, she only recently came into her own, style-wise. A few years ago, she was a big part of the club scene and had a look to match: long, streaky hair, mounds of jewelry, and skin-tight clothes. These days, she's starring in ad campaigns, wearing vintage couture gowns and fabulous designer dresses, and has become a celebrity in her own right, for just being herself. Her father, Lionel Richie, is considered music royalty, so it's only fitting that daddy's little girl has become a designer princess.

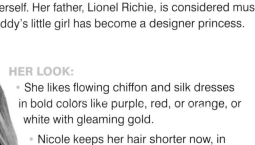

HER LOOK:

- She likes flowing chiffon and silk dresses in bold colors like purple, red, or orange, or white with gleaming gold.

- Nicole keeps her hair shorter now, in a very grown-up bob that just reaches her shoulders, that shows her more sophisticated side.

- Adding to her glamour factor, she goes everywhere wearing huge sunglasses that cover most of her face.

MANDY MOORE *Classic, with a Twist*

The thing we love most about Mandy Moore is just how amazingly normal she is. Yes, she is famous. She can act. She sings like an angel and has a face to match. But she also looks healthy and happy. She's gone from blonde to brunette, back to blonde and brunette again, but she always manages to look completely natural and glowing. She's totally at ease with herself. And her clothes—well, they're just so cute. There isn't anything shocking or particularly fashion-y about how she dresses, since she avoids flashy fads and never shows too much skin. Even off-duty, on the street in New York or at a casual event, you know that her modest (but never dorky) and flattering outfits would make any mom proud. Mandy always looks like a regular girl on her very, very best day.

HER LOOK:

- She likes to wear tank tops with skirts in the summer and jeans, boots, and sweaters in the winter. Shopping magazines are always asking her for wardrobe advice.
- She always seems like the perfect lady in sweet, full skirts or bold print dresses.
- In soft makeup and delicate jewelry, she's never overdone.

BE ALL THAT YOU CAN BE...

Which of these fashion icons can you relate to the most? Are there more than one? That's okay. You're just one person, but you can have a few different styles and look terrific in all of them. Remember, your goal is to master your own style, not copy someone else's, so it's only natural that you wouldn't rely on only one of these celebrity looks for guidance. Don't sacrifice one side of your personality for the sake of another. Here's how to combine your favorite styles.

< IF YOU LOVE SPORTY CLOTHES like hooded sweatshirts and jeans and **FLIRTY** clothes like full skirts, why not wear them together? Upgrade the sweatshirt to a long hooded sweater. You can slip it on over a dress with flip flops or sandals for cool summer nights, or throw on tights and boots and add a scarf for winter weather. Think of what Amanda Bynes does, combining a simple white tank top with a long skirt and killer heels. Or the way Sarah Jessica Parker mixes, matches, and layers.

< DO YOU HAVE A ROCK STAR EDGE AND A PREPPY SIDE? Why not wear a shrunken polo shirt with skinny black jeans tucked into boots? Or throw on a cute, fitted blazer over a rock T-shirt. Look for your preppy staples in exaggerated sizes, like a super-long striped wool scarf or a shrunken oxford from the boys department. Ashlee Simpson does it. Why can't you?

< HAVE A SOFT SPOT FOR CLASSIC CLOTHES, BUT WANT TO FIND YOUR INNER ECCENTRIC? Do what Cameron Diaz does and wear unexpected accessories to give your outfit a twist. She'll wear a simple dress with outrageous shoes, like bright turquoise sandals, or she'll carry an intricately beaded bag. Or she'll combine jeans and a tank top with a colorful shawl. Add some bold necklaces, unusual belts, and sparkly scarves to an otherwise conservative wardrobe and you'll be instantly eclectic.

< ARE YOU LONGING TO BE MORE GLAM BUT FEEL LIKE YOU'RE STUCK IN A TOMBOY RUT? Start by experimenting with different types of T-shirts: Try wearing one with a gathered waist or ties on the sleeves, or maybe even a lower, scooped neckline. Look to Keira Knightley for inspiration: she often wears jeans, but glams them up by tucking them into sleek leather boots and pairing them with a silky top or a luxe fur-lined coat. Trade in your sneakers for a pair of boots or flats once in a while, and you're well on your way to fabulous.

CLONE ALERT:
BE ONE OF A KIND

10 creative ways to stand out in a crowd

"I WEAR A UNIFORM TO SCHOOL AND IT'S HARD TO MAKE IT LOOK UNIQUE."

Can you wear colored or patterned tights or leggings under your skirt in winter? Maybe try wearing one of your Dad's ties with your button-down. Focus on fun earrings (as long as the dress code allows) or buy cute rhinestone hair clips to dress up your look. Go retro and layer a polo shirt under your oxford. Any time you get bored with your current look, don't be afraid to experiment with something new.

"EVERYONE I KNOW WEARS THE SAME SNEAKERS."

We know how it goes. While you want to look like you're in the know, you don't want to look just like everyone else. Look for a pair in a different color combination, or ones that are printed with a unusual pattern. Shoe companies' websites might have different styles than what's available at your local stores. Or check out page 85 for more ideas about how to customize your sneakers.

"MY FRIENDS ALL LOVE THE SAME STORES AND BUY THE SAME THINGS."

Layering and unique accessories are two ways to keep your look fresh. Wear two T-shirts in contrasting colors and let one peek out of the bottom. Add a vintage belt or pile on several strands of colorful plastic beads. Have fun!

"I BOUGHT A GREAT OUTFIT, ONLY TO HAVE A FRIEND GO OUT AND COPY ME!"

Unfortunately, there will always be people who have to swipe someone else's fashion sense. You know what they say: Imitation is the sincerest form of flattery. Add an unusual belt, some colorful shoes, or a one-of-a-kind necklace from a second-hand store. Or borrow something that your style-stealer can't go out and buy. If she continues to copy your every look, ask her politely to stop. Then lend her this book so she can find a look of her own!

"EVERYONE'S WEARING SKIRTS, BUT I'M MORE COMFORTABLE IN PANTS."

Try putting on a skirt with leggings (or dancer's tights without feet) underneath it, so you have the comfort and ease of pants. Cropped or wide-leg pants that flow like a skirt are another alternative. Or just skip skirts altogether and wear a longer tunic over your favorite jeans. And remember, you don't have to follow every last trend.

The color of Natasha Bedingfield's striped tights ties her outfit together.

Sienna Miller wears one-of-a-kind accessories to make every look unique.

Jessica Biel's tunic is a perfect alternative for girls who prefer pants.

WHAT'S YOUR
FASHION IQ?

Find out if you're fashion-obsessed, effortlessly fabulous, or couldn't care less.

Your idea of a perfect day is:
a) Hanging out with friends at the mall, finding a great new pair of earrings, and going to a movie
b) Plowing through store racks to find the triple-markdown jeans that have been haunting you in your sleep
c) Playing soccer, spending time with friends, and generally being as far away from the mall as possible

When you get dressed for school, you:
a) Put on one fun accessory to go with your outfit, making it look uniquely adorable
b) Try on at least a dozen things before you decide on exactly the right cuteness combo, and then tear out of the door because you're running late…again
c) Throw on whatever's clean-ish

If you see a picture of your favorite celeb looking particularly amazing, you:
a) Notice the great top she's wearing, and think that maybe you should try that color sometime
b) Study every detail of her clothing and go online to see if you can buy the boots/sunglasses/bag she's wearing
c) Glance at it, maybe show it to your friends, and then forget about it

The best part of prom is:
a) Getting all dressed up and having a big night out with your friends
b) Shopping for weeks to find the perfect dress (and then returning it when you find an even cooler one the day before)
c) The dance floor!

If you were to guess-timate the number of pairs of jeans in your closet, it would be closest to:
a) Seven, but it could be more like five
b) No guessing—you've got exactly 16 pairs
c) Three, and that's rounding up

Your favorite types of movies are:
a) Classics and independent releases
b) Chick flicks with big-name stars
c) Action-packed blockbusters

The most important function that your handbag needs to perform is:
a) Holding your stuff while looking cute
b) Being the finishing touch for your look, even if that means it only holds your lip gloss and house key
c) Handbag? You mean backpack, right?

Uggs are:
a) Comfy and good for knocking around
b) So last year (unless they are customized)
c) The grunts that little trolls make

The saying "fashionably late" means:
a) Arriving about 20 minutes after everyone else
b) Showing up when everyone's already there in order to make sure all eyes are on you when you make your grand entrance
c) You're "officially" late, but no one is bugged about it

Off the playing field and out of the gym, you wear sneakers:
a) Sometimes, depending on your mood
b) When you're going for a "sporty casual" look
c) All the time

If you see someone walking down the street and you like her skirt, you:
a) Compliment her and make a mental note
b) Stop her in her tracks, tell her you love her skirt, ask her who makes it and where she bought it
c) Smile and think maybe you should try wearing skirts more often

You go to a party on Saturday night. Your friend shows up wearing the same shrunken blazer. You:
a) Go up to her and compliment her awesome taste
b) Confront her and demand that she take the jacket off—you got there first!
c) Who cares? It's just a jacket.

Your score . . .

If your answers were mostly A's...

You're stylish but not obsessed with fashion, and you don't need to follow every trend that comes along. Shopping can also be a blast, but it doesn't take up your entire life (or all of your spending money, for that matter). You probably relate to more relaxed style icons, like **Jessica Alba** or **Mischa Barton**. Every once in a while, for a special occasion or a big night, you'll let loose and show your inner glamour goddess.

If your answers were mostly B's...

You should probably be writing this book! You know all of the designers' names and which celebrity wore whose dress at which awards show. You pore over fashion magazines and never miss a sale at your favorite store. Getting dressed is always a major event, and you've been known to organize your outfits the night before so you don't run late—again. You share **Paris Hilton's** trend obsession, have an accessories collection that could rival **Nicole Richie's,** and admire **Beyoncé** for her nonstop glitz. Just be careful not to go overboard—fashion should be fun!

If your answers were mostly C's...

You think "Juicy" is a word that describes oranges. For you, a day at the mall that doesn't involve a movie is wasted time. Your idea of dressing up is wearing a clean T-shirt and your best jeans...and maybe wearing shoes that don't have laces. Your style icon? No question: **Missy Elliott.** Look to stylish tomboys like Missy, **Michelle Rodriguez,** or **Drew Barrymore** for fun dress-up ideas—no ruffles or strappy sandals required!

2 BODY

BASICS

Knowing your shape and learning how to dress to accentuate your best features is the number-one celebrity style secret.

BODIES COME IN ALL SHAPES

Celebrities really look just like the rest of us. The difference between "them" and "us" is that they have a paid team of experts whose job it is to make them look as perfect as possible for the camera, including a wardrobe person or stylist who has taught them how to dress for the shape they've got. Find your shape in the following pages and learn the wardrobe tips and tricks that every star knows.

TALL

LIKE
MAGGIE
GRACE

PETITE

LIKE
BRITTANY
MURPHY

CURVY ON
TOP

LIKE
LINDSAY
LOHAN

No two are just alike

CURVY ON THE BOTTOM	CURVY ALL OVER	STRAIGHT UP AND DOWN	BROAD SHOULDERED

LIKE ASHANTI	LIKE RAVEN	LIKE KIRSTEN DUNST	LIKE JESSICA ALBA

THE PERFECTION MYTH

What's the point in wishing you were built differently? There will always be curvy girls who want to be flatter, women with less on top who want more, tall people who want to be shorter, and petite people who long to be lanky. Why not realize that you are who you are and make the most of it? Here's the truth: no body's perfect.

6 SIMPLE RULES FOR DRESSING YOUR BEST

1) Amy Adams clearly feels good about her shoulders.

1) Hilarie Burton is proud of her shapely legs.

These guidelines apply to everyone, regardless of your body type.

1 **Call attention to the parts you really like.** If you think you have pretty arms, wear sleeveless tops and tanks, dresses with spaghetti straps, or slim-fitting long sleeves when it's colder. Love your legs, but not your arms? Wear a loose-fitting top and slim-fitting jeans or a short skirt. Do you want to show off your slim waist? Try a wraparound T-shirt or dress that accentuates your middle.

2 **Use color to your advantage.** Brightly colored clothing makes parts stand out, while dark colors help them hide a little. If you're curvy on top and you want to downplay that, wear a black T-shirt paired with white jeans or a pink skirt. If you're curvy on the bottom and you'd rather highlight your top, wear a bright top and black pants or dark jeans.

3 **The neater, the better.** Slightly scuffed shoes may look cooler than brand-new ones, and frayed jeans have a certain appeal. But filthy jeans and shoes that are falling apart are a different story entirely.

Imagine the most perfect-looking person you can think of, and, chances are, she has a complaint or two about her body. No one ever really thinks she's flawless, but that doesn't keep her from smiling for the camera anyway.

Simple tricks like wearing fabrics that don't cling to your curves and avoiding clothes that have bulky seams can make a huge difference.

You don't need to be taller, shorter, more or less curvy to look stylishly turned out. You only need to know how to work it. Just think, if you feel more comfortable in your clothes every day, then maybe, just maybe, you'll feel more comfortable with your body, too.

3) A tangerine sweater calls attention to Alicia Keys' slim waist.

Jennifer Love Hewitt knows how important good posture is.

4 **Cheap clothes reveal their price in the way they fit.** It's great to grab a bargain when you can, but for fit, it's sometimes better to spend a little bit more. The seams of super-cheap pants aren't sewn very well, so they can pull and bunch up and make you look bulkier than you are. The best bargains are loose-fitting, trendy clothes that aren't built to last more than a few months anyway.

5 **Horizontal equals wide, vertical equals long.** This is a pretty simple rule to remember. Sideways stripes, like on a rugby shirt, make areas look wider. Up and down stripes, like pin stripes, make parts look longer and leaner. Pin-striped pants make sense if you want your legs to look longer. And if you have a long waist and shorter legs, stay way from vertical-striped shirts. Horizontal stripes make a big chest look even bigger.

6 **Stand up straight.** It's old news, but it's true—good posture makes everything you wear look better. Slouching makes even the most amazing outfit look sloppy.

HOW TO DRESS FOR YOUR BODY TYPE

IF YOU'RE **TALL**... *like Mischa Barton*

It can be hard towering over your friends, standing in the back row of every picture, or having to crouch down a little to whisper in a cute guy's ear. But the pluses really outnumber the minuses, especially when it comes to clothes. Mischa Barton is taller than almost all of her TV costars, but you don't catch her slumping in the corner. She likes above-the-knee skirts and minidresses (to emphasize her long legs) and sleek, pointy-toe flats.

THE ABC'S OF... JEANS AND PANTS

- Tall girls, for the most part, can wear whatever the heck they want, and they almost never have to shorten their pants. These days, jeans and pants are available with different lengths of inseams (and anything with an "L" next to the size is a tall girl's best friend), so fit isn't much of a problem.

- Have you grown out of all your pants? Wear them intentionally short. Jeans cut off just above the ankle, worn with flats, boots, heels, or simple

Anne Hathaway

sneakers, can be very flattering on long legs.

- If your legs are super-skinny, don't make the mistake of wearing overly baggy jeans. They can make you look even thinner, like you're swimming in your clothes (and a little sloppier). Try jeans in your size that are snug around your butt.

- Make your backside look bigger with smaller back

pockets, or look smaller with regular-sized or large pockets. It's the contrast in size that does it.

- For wider legs and hips, wide-leg pants and jeans that are fitted near the top and get wider at the bottom are most flattering.

SKIRTS

- Miniskirts call attention to long legs, which is great if you want it! But showing a lot of skin can be uncomfortable. The trick is to choose either shorter OR tighter—not short and tight together. To counteract all of that skin showing on your lower half, try a miniskirt with a looser-fitting top with short or long sleeves, or cover up with a short jacket.

- Watch the length of long skirts. A skirt or dress that stops at the thickest part of your calf can look frumpy and especially awkward on tall frames. Extra-long skirts should graze the top of your shoes, not hit the floor.

- If you're long and extra-lean, add curves to your frame with a pencil skirt—a straight, fitted skirt that hits at the knee.

- A-line skirts that flare out just above the knee can make curves look slimmer, or narrow hips look curvier.

JACKETS AND TOPS

- Too-short T-shirts are a tall girl's worst nightmare. Look for styles that hit at the hips—or at least cover your waistband—to avoid belly- and back-baring.

Rosario Dawson

Katharine Heigl

- If you're extra-long-waisted (your body seems longer than your legs), try a shorter jacket, like a cropped bomber, or a cropped sweater over a longer T-shirt, to balance the length of your torso with the length of your legs.

- For narrow shoulders, try a jean jacket or a boy blazer to make them seem broader. Also, tops with details at the shoulder (gathered, beaded, or tied) can help balance the look of small shoulders with the rest of a tall frame.

- Try wearing an oversize sweater that drops down to the hips or below: If you can't pull that off, tall girl, nobody can!

Mischa Barton

DRESSES

- Avoid short baby-doll dresses; they can look out of proportion on taller frames. Longer empire-waist dresses, however, can look elegant.

- If you're long and lean, try a bold pattern to help create curves. If you want to feel a little slimmer, try a solid, dark color dress that hits at the knee.

- Add a belt or a silky sash to a solid-color dress to break up the line if you feel like a single color from top to toe makes you look even longer.

TIP: Tall people can wear layers without looking like they're being swallowed up by their clothes. Look at the way Paris Hilton piles on accessories! Try adding a long scarf and a strand of beads or two. Your tall frame can handle it.

IF YOU'RE PETITE... *like Rachel Bilson*

Nicole Richie

If you're short, don't sweat it. Smaller people, like Rachel Bilson, can fit into vintage clothes better...and pull off the occasional platform wedge sandal better than anybody. To us, these sound like good enough reasons to be psyched about being short.

THE ABC'S OF... JEANS AND PANTS

- Do you know how to sew? If not, it might be a good idea to learn. Hemming pants and jeans is a big part of being tiny. If that's not an option, ask your local dry cleaner if they do alterations—hemming pants can cost as little as $5. Bear in mind: If you know you're going to have to alter something to make it look right on you, you need to mentally add in the potential cost before you decide to buy it.
- Avoid cropped jeans or pants. They cut off your leg mid-calf and can subtract from the height you have.
- Choose straight or skinny jeans that are a bit longer so they cover most of the back of your shoe to create a lean, tall line.
- Really baggy jeans are a no-go. They can make you look wider, stocky, and bulky, like you're wearing hand-me-downs that don't quite fit your small frame.
- Same with pleated pants. They add width at your waistline and emphasize your small stature just a little too much.

SKIRTS

- Miniskirts can look terrific on a small frame. Legs look long and lanky in dark tights under minis in winter, or bare with sandals in the summer because of all of that exposed skin. In general, the miniskirt-and-sneaker combination makes legs look short and stocky, which is not what you're going for.
- Longer skirts can create a flowing line, as long as there's not too much fabric. Overly gathered or tiered skirts can look like they weigh down a small frame, dragging it to the ground. Try a lightweight, loosely draped skirt that hits at the lower calf, above the ankle, for the best results.
- A-line skirts (which flare out a little at the knee)

Hilary Duff

work for virtually any body type. Pair them with close-fitting tops and you can't go wrong.
- The same goes for fuller skirts: Make sure they hit at the knee or shorter, and balance out the fullness on the bottom with a smaller, snug top so your clothes don't take over your shape.

JACKETS AND TOPS

- Try shorter jackets that hit above the hip or at the waist, with just one or two buttons. Long shapes that hit right at the hip can drag you down.
- Closer-fitting tops are usually more flattering on petite bodies than big, blousy shirts, but there are some exceptions. If you do choose an oversize shirt, make sure that some skin is showing, like a shoulder or your forearms, so it doesn't look like your petite frame is completely wrapped in fabric.
- Higher waistlines, like a baby doll or an empire waist that starts just below the chest, can make you look and feel a little taller.
- Toss long, droopy sweaters or anything that makes you feel like you're wearing clothes made for a bigger person.

DRESSES

- If you want to wear a long dress to a special occasion, choose one that's long and straight or A-line, not full. A full, floor-length skirt can be too much fabric for a smaller person. If you want to feel like a princess in a full skirt, make sure it's knee-length or tea-length (just above the ankle) for the most flattering effect.

- Play with the proportions: A long-sleeve dress should have a shorter skirt, while a strapless or sleeveless bodice can bal-ance out a longer bottom half. Once again, a lot of fabric is not a good idea for someone who is on the small side.

- Since vintage dresses are almost always tiny, scour secondhand stores for fun, one-of-a-kind dresses at bargain prices.

Eva Longoria

TIP: If you're comfortable wearing heels, go for it! A wedge-soled shoe or a casual boot is a good choice for daytime and school, when comfort is key. But don't feel as though you have to.

Mena Suvari

Rachel Bilson

IF YOU'RE CURVY ON TOP...
like Scarlett Johanssen

Scarlett Johanssen

Magazine ads, billboards, and television commercials are filled with women who want to show off their curves. So it's hard for some people to believe that women who've got it don't always want to flaunt it. We know how hard it can be to find clothes that don't cling or make you uncomfortable, and no one should have to hide under a sweatshirt. No matter what your bra size, there's no reason to be ashamed of your figure, or to have to hide it. If you know how to dress for your shape like Scarlett Johanssen does, then having a fuller chest doesn't have to be an issue at all.

THE ABC's OF... JEANS AND PANTS

- If you'd like to deflect attention from a larger top, move the focus downward. If you want to experiment with colors or patterns without attracting attention to your curves, wear them on your bottom half, like cords in a bold color or pin-striped pants.

- Cinching your waist or tucking in your shirts can emphasize the difference in size between your waist and your bustline. Wear skinny belts instead of

Erika Christensen

chunky ones, and pants that can be worn without a tucked-in shirt.

- When you wear looser shirts, keep your pants slim-fitting. Proportions are important: Wearing baggy clothes from head to toe will look frumpy, and like you're trying too hard to hide your shape.

SKIRTS

- Draw attention away from your upper body with a colorful or patterned skirt.

- If you have slimmer hips, show them off with a pencil skirt paired with a looser top.

Carmen Electra

- Proportions are key. If you have a loose-fitting or gathered top, don't wear a loose-fitting gathered skirt. If you're wearing a loose top, go for a straight skirt or an A-line skirt that tapers out from the waist and stops at the knee.

JACKETS AND TOPS

- Woven cotton shirts, like button-down oxfords, are difficult for girls with curvy tops. If it fits around the chest, it'll probably be loose and baggy everywhere else, or vice versa. Avoid them altogether, or have them taken in at the waist. If you do wear a button-down top, make sure that the fabric doesn't pull and leave gaps between the buttons.
- Ruffles or pleats around the neckline only add bulk and busyness to an area

you don't need to attract more attention to. Instead, go for smooth, simple tops, with a simple neckline, like a shallow v- or scoop neck.

- If you're tired of covering up, subtle cleavage can be really pretty. Try wearing a henley or a blousy shirt that crisscrosses in the front.

Meagan Good

- High crewneck T-shirts can also call unwelcome attention to a larger chest. Look for a medium scoop neck or a wide boatneck that shows a little shoulder instead.
- Cropped sweaters that are gathered at the waist will also make your top look heavier. Try some that don't have a band around the waist, and fall neatly over the waistband of your pants.

DRESSES

- Dresses are the hardest clothes to fit into if you're curvy on top. What fits on the bottom may be too tight on the top, or the other way around. Fabrics that have a little stretch are more forgiving. Wrap dresses can accommodate a curvier top.
- If you want to show a little more skin, a generously cut triangular halter dress that fastens around the neck shows off your shoulders and covers up cleavage. Look for one in a soft fabric that drapes softly to the waist.
- Remember proportions. If you choose to wear a long-sleeve dress, try one with a

Angelina Jolie

Drew Barrymore

slightly scooped neckline or one that is cut above the knees so you're not covered up entirely. A dress that has both long sleeves and a long skirt should skim along your body, and not be too baggy. Showing a little skin or calling attention to some of your curves keeps it from looking too dowdy.

TIP: The good news is that you don't have to work too hard to look cute and sexy. Your feminine shape makes even the subtlest clothes look ladylike. If you're comfortable enough to call attention to your shape, go for it! If not, keep your top half streamlined and simple (with solid tops and sleek jackets) and add the details on the bottom (like a ruffled skirt, bright shoes, or patterned tights).

IF YOU'RE CURVY ON THE BOTTOM . . .
like Jennifer Lopez

Why girls and women continue to stress out about having a curvy bottom half is a mystery. As Jennifer Lopez knows, having curves on the bottom is part of the fun of being a woman. It can be hard to find extra-skinny designer jeans to suit your proportions, but that's where denim with a little stretch makes all the difference. It's not hard to find a look that flatters your curviness and stick to it.

THE ABC's OF... JEANS AND PANTS

- If you don't want to emphasize the width of your hips, don't wear pants that taper down to the ankles. Very narrow-legged pants show the width difference between your hips, knees, and ankles. Instead, choose a boot cut or flared pair (that's fitted through the leg and slightly flared at the bottom) to create a more balanced shape.

- Super-low-rise jeans and pants don't always cover up a fuller bottom half. And no one wants to walk around town with her undies and backside exposed to the world.

Choose jeans that have a low-to-medium rise, not too high-waisted or too low, for the most flattering fit.

- Dark-washed denim and pants in solid dark colors like chocolate brown or navy keep your rear and legs looking slender. Save light colors, prints and patterns for your top half.

- Pockets can add additional bulk. Remember to keep your pockets empty whenever possible. Even your keys and a lipgloss can add extra bulk. If you find that the fabric of the pocket bunches up too much, sew the opening closed and cut out the

Beyoncé

rest. Or have a tailor remove it so your legs look more streamlined.

- Try pants without back pockets for a smoother look. With jeans, make sure that the pockets aren't too small. A curvy butt can seem even curvier when it's compared to tiny pockets! Avoid front pockets or patches that tend to make hips look wider.

SKIRTS

- Miniskirts can be tricky if you want to draw attention away from your lower curves. If you decide to wear one, make sure it is loose enough not to stretch or cut into your waist or hips. Try it with dark tights and flats, or low-heeled boots. In the summer, a knee-length skirt with a little fullness and bare legs with flat-strappy sandals may be more flattering.

- Pleated skirts that are fitted around the waist and abdomen and begin to flare out at the hips, can be a good option for flattering curves. A-line skirts that hit at the knee look great on you, too.

- Long skirts can add even more bulk to your lower half, especially tiered skirts that hug your hips

Natasha Bedingfield

and thighs and flare out again at the bottom. Tulip-shaped skirts, also called mermaid (which are fitted through the butt, hips, and thighs and begin to flare out at the knee), exaggerate anyone's shape, but especially anyone with a curvy lower half.

- Avoid odd pockets or extra details around the hips and thighs that could add bulk.

JACKETS AND TOPS

- Any kind of extra detail—a ruffle, gathers, beading, decorative buttons—should be saved for your top half.

- Experiment with fun tops that accentuate your favorite parts, like your arms and shoulders or collarbone, to keep eyes focused above the waist.

- Cropped or short-waisted tops and jackets can also expose your lower curves in an unflattering way. Your jackets and sweaters should hit at your waistband or just below. A cardigan or jacket that's low enough to graze your hips can add extra bulk.

Mya

DRESSES

- With dresses, if the top fits, the bottom is often too snug, or the other way around. Look for dresses in a knit fabric that gives a little but is thick enough not to be too clingy.

- A dress that has a looser fit, and is more revealing on the top, is a good

Jennifer Lopez

choice. Spaghetti straps and a formfitting bodice, lower waist and a fuller skirt is the ideal shape for this body type.

- A 1940s shape, with fuller shoulders and that skims along the waist and hips, can also be flattering because it balances the upper- and lower-body proportions well.

Eva Mendes

TIP: Denim designers add pockets and seams to create shape for women with less curvy frames! Take advantage of your curvy shape by wearing more feminine, less boyish clothes. Shakira loves her hips so much that she ties a string of bells around her waist to call attention to them! We're not recommending you go that far, but don't feel like you have to hide them, either.

IF YOU'RE CURVY ALL OVER...

like Raven

To have a figure with curves on top and on the bottom is womanly, and something you can be very proud of, like Raven is. The trick is to balance your top half with your bottom half, and seek out clothes that enhance slender waists, lovely legs, and slim arms.

THE ABC's OF... JEANS AND PANTS

- Wear jeans that are made for girls and women, that are built to fit actual curves. Boy-cut pants are for straight-up-and-down bodies, and will be too snug in the hips, or too loose in the waist, and generally uncomfortable.

- Because your curves are proportional (you've got them on top and on the bottom), you can play with cuts and lengths of pants without much trouble. Try capri jeans, or cropped jeans with a cuff, in a fabric that has a tiny bit of stretch so it's snug where you need it to be without being restrictive. The details at the bottom (a cuff or exposed ankles and cute shoes) keep everything in balance from top to toe.

- Pleated pants create more volume around the hips, so stay away from those. Instead, try flat front pants with a wider leg, either full-length or cropped below the knee.

- The same goes for high-waisted pants. If you're curvy, they can exaggerate the difference between your waist and your hips, or they can cut into your middle and be uncomfortable to wear.

- Consider buying one size larger if you don't want a skintight fit that can exaggerate a curvy frame (just don't forget a belt).

- Make sure your pockets don't add additional bulk, and keep them empty

Amber Tamblyn

Raven

when you can. If you find that the fabric of the pocket bunches up too much, sew it together near the opening and cut out the rest. Or have a tailor remove it so your leg look is more streamlined.

- With jeans, make sure that the back pockets aren't too small. A curvy rear can look even curvier when it's compared to tiny pockets! Avoid front pockets or patches that tend to make hips look wider.

- If you have a slender waist and want to show it off, go for it. Add an interesting belt or a sash that fits snugly but isn't too tight. If your waist is thicker, a thin belt works best.

SKIRTS

- A wrap skirt is great for a curvy frame because it can be adjusted to your waistline and is roomier in the hips.

- Soft, drapey styles with no obvious waistband are also flattering. Look for fabrics that are soft and skim over your curves instead of clinging to them.

- Vertical seams or stitching can help make your bottom half look longer and leaner. Horizontal details can do the opposite.

- If your waist is thicker, avoid skirts with waistbands that can cut into it and make you uncomfortable. If you want to show off your waist, add a belt or a sash.

- Flat-front styles with a zipper on the side or the back give you a smoother look in front.

JACKETS AND TOPS

- Button-up shirts in woven fabric, like cotton oxford shirts, can be hard to wear if you have curves on the top. If it fits around the chest, it might be loose and baggy everywhere else. Once again, don't shop in the guys' department. If you can find a shirt that's made to accommodate curves, make sure you buy a size large enough so the buttons don't pull or strain.

- Ruffles or pleats around the neckline only add bulk and busy details to an area that doesn't need to attract more attention. Look for vertical details

America Fererra

like stitching, seams, or thin stripes instead.

- If you're tired of covering up, subtle cleavage can be really pretty. Try wearing a lower-cut tank top under a deep V-neck sweater, or a blousy shirt that crisscrosses in the front.

- High crewneck T-shirts can also call unwelcome attention to a larger chest. Try a medium scoop neck, or a wide boatneck that shows a little shoulder, instead.

- Short, cropped sweaters that are gathered at the waist may make your top look heavier. Also avoid baggy, shapeless tops. They will give you a rounder, apple shape instead of a curvy, hourglass form.

DRESSES

- Wrap dresses are made for girls who are curvy all over, since you tie them to show off your waist and can adjust the fit to suit your shape.

- Don't try to hide your curves under a shapeless, baggy dress that covers all of your skin, which will just add bulk to your frame. Instead, try a sleeveless dress that shows off your arms, or a shorter skirt that draws the focus to slender legs.

- Choose dresses with details in areas that you'd like people to notice, like sleeves with embroidery, or an interesting ruffled edge around cuffs or the hemline.

Queen Latifah

- Stay away from cinched-waist dresses, or anything with a big belt or a sash, if you don't want to call attention to your middle section. A shift dress, which is straighter up and down, or something cut on the bias (which flows a little and just skims over your curves) are better choices.

TIP: Everything looks better with the right underwear. Take the time to find a bra that fits well, gives enough support, and doesn't create bulges in the back or front. (Most department stores have someone to fit you in the lingerie department.) The same goes for undies. Find pairs that don't have obvious seams or elastic around the legs for a smooth look.

IF YOU'RE STRAIGHT UP AND DOWN . . .

like Selma Blair

Narrow figures like yours are a designer's dream. Those of us with straighter shapes, like Selma Blair, can wear just about anything, and creating curves can be as easy as cinching a wide belt around your waist, wearing a puffy-sleeve blouse, or sporting well-fitting cropped pants. Having a boyish figure around people with newly formed curves can be troubling at first, but once you get used to dressing to enhance your shape, you'll be grateful for your lean frame.

Cameron Diaz

THE ABC'S OF... JEANS AND PANTS

- Skinny or boy-cut jeans and pants and long, lean cords are made for bodies like yours. Cuffed and cropped styles are flattering, too. Almost anything goes, except for baggy, which can make your shape look and feel more squared off than it is.

- Look for flap pockets in the back, or interesting stitching which may help create the look of curves.

- If your rear is flatter than you'd like it to be, buy jeans in a slightly stretchy fabric. The snugger the fit, the better.

DRESSES

- Soft, draping fabric; bright colors; fun patterns; and lots ot details can make you look shapelier.

- A V-neck dress with a full skirt makes your slim frame look curvier.

- One-shoulder and asymmetrical shapes can also make curves look softer and, well, curvier.

Claire Danes

Selma Blair

JACKETS AND TOPS

- Anything that gathers or cinches at the waist creates curves. Look for wraparound T-shirts, or tops that are tailored to fit your torso. The same goes for belted jackets and shirts and deep V-necks.

- Details at the shoulders— like beading, appliqués, or ties—can make them appear broader, and your waist smaller.

- Horizontal patterns can really make your curves look curvier. So can front pockets and detailing, like a western-style shirt.

- Stay away from square necklines (like a tank top that's cut straight across with straps)—they can make your top look flatter and more narrow.

Keira Knightley

Ginnifer Goodwin

SKIRTS

- Just about any style of skirt can be flattering on you, so have fun experimenting with pencil skirts, minis, full skirts, or A-lines.

- Pleats and gathers at the waistline can make your bottom half seem curvier.

- Try a bold pattern or print on the bottom. You don't have anything you need to hide, so go for it.

TIP: Take advantage of your lean, narrow frame by choosing wide butterfly sleeves, off-the-shoulder tops—just about anything can add more shape to your shape.

IF YOU'RE **BROAD-SHOULDERED . . .**
like Jessica Biel

Anna Kournikova

People often call this a swimmer's or an athlete's body, because broad shoulders signify strength. If you're concerned that yours might be too broad, look to Jessica Biel for inspiration—she's one of the fittest women in Hollywood. Broader shoulders also balance out your lower half to create a leaner look. Soft, pretty necklines, drapey tops, and delicate fabrics can make broader shoulders seem slightly more feminine.

THE ABC'S OF... JEANS AND PANTS

• Since people with broad shoulders often have slim hips, too, try looking for jeans and pants with horizontal details, like bold stitching on the front pockets, or pockets with flaps (on the front or the back), to balance your proportions.

• If your hips aren't really narrow, stick with slim-fitting pants that are boot cut (slightly flared at the bottom) to keep things simple and in proportion.

SKIRTS

• Stay away from super-full skirts, which can make your body seem broad on the bottom, too. Instead, try an A-line skirt that gradually flares from the waist to the knee or a softly draping style with just a little fullness.

• If you have narrow hips, try a skirt with a horizontal stripe or pattern to give the illusion of curves and make your frame look more balanced.

JACKETS AND TOPS

• If you want to make your shoulders look slightly softer, look for longer tops and jackets that are loose or drapey and fall below the waist.

• Interesting bell-shaped or dolman sleeves (that are wider than your arm and drape downward) also help to soften a broad upper body.

• If you don't want to draw attention to your shoulders, choose smaller collars and jackets with

Jessica Alba

Jennifer Garner

skinny lapels, not large ones that cover a lot of your chest and point outward.

• Deep V-necks can make your upper body look longer and de-emphasize broad shoulders, while halter tops that tie at the neck exaggerate broad shoulders.

• Stay away from puffy sleeves and anything that adds bulk to your upper arms.

• Wear dark colors on top (which makes an area seem smaller) and light colors on bottom (which takes up most of the attention) if you want to make your upper body seem slimmer.

DRESSES

- Dresses with puffy or pronounced sleeves only exaggerate the shape of your shoulders, so it's smart to avoid those. Try sleeveless styles instead, or a long sleeve with a straight, simple, shoulder-pad-free shape.

- It might be tempting to try to balance out a broad upper body with a very full skirt, but resist the urge. Proportionally, it looks a little awkward. Try a soft, draping dress with a few gathers at the waist instead.

- Take advantage of your narrow hips by wearing a simple shift dress: It has no waistband, just a few darts along the bodice, and falls just to the knee. Shifts are classic and usually sleeveless, and since they're about the same width from the shoulder to the knee (just a little narrower at the waist), it can give the appearance of more balance between your shoulders and your hips. Curvier shapes can rarely pull off this cute, timeless style, so go for it, if you can.

- Wrap dresses that cross the body can point out the broadness of your upper body. Try a simple V-neck dress instead.

TIP: If you love your broad shoulders, show them off! Wear delicate tank tops or strapless dresses that highlight your strong, beautiful body. It wasn't that long ago that practically every shirt and jacket in the stores had pads in them to make shoulders more prominent, so be proud that you don't need any extra help.

Jessica Biel

3 COLORS,

PATTERNS
+PRINTS

A Crash Course

PICKING PERFECT PATTERNS

Whether it's a skirt length, the shape of a sleeve, or the colors and patterns you choose—these days, the best part about fashion and trends is that almost anything goes. Practically nothing is off-limits (except maybe giant polka dots, which will make anybody look like a clown). In fact, layering patterns and coming up with unexpected color combinations are two great ways to stretch your wardrobe and give yourself dozens more outfit options without setting foot in a store. A single patterned shirt can be worn at least 6 different ways.

THE RULE OF 6
ONE CUTE, PRINTED CAMISOLE

1. Goes under a jacket with a denim skirt or jeans.

2. Pairs really well with dressy pants and a hooded sweatshirt tossed over it.

3. Looks sweet worn over a ribbed tank top with a summery cotton skirt.

4. Is cool layered over a short-sleeve vintage-y T-shirt or under a menswear-inspired vest with jeans and a scarf.

5. Looks hip over a long-sleeve thermal shirt (and think about adding a jacket or a cardigan).

6. Is an ideal choice on its own or under a beaded cardigan for night.

Carmen Electra knows how to dress up a camisole tons of different ways. She looks summery and sweet wearing it with a sweater and knee-length shorts; and a little edgy and sexy when pairing it with a men's vest and jeans.

AND SHADES

that were made for you

THE RULE OF 6
ONE PATTERNED SHORT-SLEEVE COLLARED SHIRT

1. Goes under a jacket like **Jessica Alba's** with jeans, pants, or skirts.

2. Dresses up a crewneck sweatshirt, layered underneath with the collar peeking out.

3. Works well with a V-neck sweater, when more of the pattern is exposed.

4. Is completely cute layered under a sweater vest.

5. Is totally cool layered over a long-sleeve henley or thermal shirt.

6. Is perfect all by itself (maybe cinched with a belt, if it's long enough).

Patterns can take on a lot of different personalities: A plaid kilt can be preppy or punky, depending on what accessories you wear with it. And just one little item with an of-the-moment print can be an immediate wardrobe update that doesn't break the bank. Mixing patterns is yet another way to express your personality.

When it comes to color, trust your instincts. If you try on that bright yellow sweater and it makes you look like a giant banana (or worse: like you're car sick) then you're probably not going to buy it. Maybe a butter yellow or pale daffodil might look better on you. Still no good? Skip it and buy the blue one.

Read on for more information about your astrological color match, how to choose the shade that's right for you, what prints say about your personality, and more.

THEY'RE TRENDY— IN A GOOD WAY

There are some seasons when it seems like every piece of clothing in every store is covered with the same style of print—butterflies, camouflage, leopard, you name it. At first, it's tempting to gobble up as much of the pattern as you can because it looks so fresh. But resist the urge to splurge! Instead, find just one item in that pattern that you absolutely love that's not too pricey. These things can go out of style just as fast as they came in, and if you've invested in a super-expensive dress (not to mention an entire wardrobe), it will look dated in a month. When the trend is over, you will have gotten major mileage out of that piece and won't be left with a closet full of expensive things you wore only a few times before the fashion moment was over. Amanda Peet knows how to incorporate trendy pieces (like this jacket) into her wardrobe while the trend is hot.

THEY MAKE GREAT ACCESSORIES

Aah, the beauty of bags: Even if you're not a full-time preppy stripes/girly flowers/funky ethnic-print person, you can experiment in small doses with a belt, a scarf, or even a canvas bag in the season's trendiest prints. Brittany Snow spices up an all-black ensemble with her boldly printed bag.

PRINTS ARE THE INSTANT MESSAGES OF THE FASHION WORLD

More than the color or cut of clothes, they say who you are. For example: An argyle sweater, which has diamonds and lines in a traditional Scottish pattern, is automatic preppy. A graffiti print is a little bit hip-hop or punk. The colors you wear change according to your skin tone and color. And the fit of the clothes you wear has more to do with your body type and what fabrics and shapes work best on you than your style. But patterns are chosen because of your style and your style alone. Christina Ricci follows the guidlines for her petite, curvy-on-top frame, but the leopard print is a style statement all her own.

THEY MAKE IT EASY TO SWITCH UP YOUR STYLE

Maybe you're a prepster who's thinking about giving the boho thing a go? Buy an Indian-print or embroidered scarf and use it as a headband, tie it on the handle of your bag, or wrap it around your waist to make a belt. When it comes to experimenting with new things, it's best to start slowly with accessories and build up if it feels right. It's also an easy way to update your look. Zoe Saldana adds a Bohemian touch to her very ladylike shirtdress with the paisley scarf tied around her waist.

SPLIT-PERSONALITY PRINTS

Prints, like people, have different sides to their personalities, and a print's scale can reflect how you're feeling on a given day, whether it's sporty, ladylike, preppy, or punk. Let this cheat sheet be your guide.

HORIZONTAL STRIPES generally say... SPORTY
Big, horizontal stripes on sweaters, rugbys, or polo shirts are nearly always sporty. On a narrower scale, they're nautical or collegiate.

THIN VERTICAL STRIPES which say... TAILORED
Pinstripes on dark fabric, which first appeared on men's business suits, are about as sophisticated as you can get. Now, they pop up on just about anything and always look timeless. Striped oxfords and seersucker, a summer-weight cotton with a slightly rough texture, are also thin-striped classics.

Meagan Good

VS.

Jennifer Aniston

LARGE FLORAL PRINTS mostly say... LADYLIKE
Big, colorful flowers look right at home on flowing dresses, full skirts, and prim blouses. It doesn't take much fabric to make a big impact, so a halter top or a miniskirt may be all the blooms you need to make a statement.

SMALL FLORAL PRINTS, which generally say... ARTSY
Miniature flower prints on long-sleeve cotton tunics, camisoles, or tiered skirts, of fabrics made in foreign countries like India, Thailand, or Indonesia, have a creative, artistic flair. They're feminine, but they're also free-spirited.

Penelope Cruz

VS.

Amy Adams

TRADITIONAL PLAIDS say... PREPPY OR PUNKY

Trad plaids are a school uniform staple that can also be a little bit radical. Punk-rock pioneers in London ripped apart traditional plaids and pieced them back together with safety pins as a sign of rebellion.

Rachel Bilson

VS.

Jennifer Lopez

SMALL PLAIDS, which say... COUNTRY

Western shirts make good use of plaids, and have a timeless quality that can look good on anyone, regardless of their style (but they look especially dashing on cowboys). Gingham checks have a country, picnic-blanket feel to them—in a good way.

BOLD ETHNIC PRINTS can say...BOHEMIAN

If you want to make a statement that you're eccentric, try large, ethnic prints inspired by or made in places like Africa, China, or Japan. They say that you're into looking to other cultures for style cues and aren't afraid to draw a little attention your way.

Claire Danes

VS.

Paris Hilton

SMALL ETHNIC PRINTS, which generally say...FEMME

Stitched details, embroidery, and beading have been appreciated by girls who love feminine details for hundreds of years. On Mexican cotton dresses or puffy sleeve blouses from Russia, these handmade details add a special, dainty touch to any outfit.

BOLD GRAPHIC PRINTS generally say...MODERN

Giant letters, prints of faces, artists' drawings, or logos make a strong, modern statement that you are not afraid to be noticed. No matter what item they're on, graphic prints always make a big impact.

Nicole Richie

VS.

Zooey Deschanel

SMALL GRAPHIC PRINTS, which usually say...VINTAGE

Tiny patterns have an old-fashioned quality to them, like a black-and-white movie. These vintage patterns have a way of being reinvented year after year.

WHAT'S YOUR PRINT PERSONALITY?

Answer these questions to see which pattern suits your style:

1. The Rachel McAdams character I'm most like is
a) Allie Hamilton in *The Notebook*: a 1940s glamour girl
b) Regina George in *Mean Girls*: a miniskirt-wearing modern diva
c) Claire Cleary in *The Wedding Crashers*: a social worker and environmentalist with a preppy past
d) Amy Stone in *The Family Stone*: the rebel sister who lives in rock T-shirts

2. My idea of the perfect date is
a) The works: going to nice dinner and a school dance with a corsage on my wrist
b) A quick bite at a loud restaurant where all of my friends are hanging out, and then going to the multiplex to see a comedy on a huge screen
c) A long walk, or an even longer conversation about my favorite book over organic coffee or herbal tea
d) Going to see my favorite band, then yelling to each other on the ride home since we're practically deaf from the music

3. The family member's closet I'd most like to raid is
a) My fashionable grandmother's, because she's saved all of her old dresses
b) My stylish cousin's, because she lives in Los Angeles and wants to be an actress
c) My older sister's, who won't wear fur and is into animal rights
d) My punk-rock older brother's, for his collection of Ramones T-shirts

4. Your favorite sweaters are
a) Cardigans, some with beads or sequins around the neckline
b) In bright colors, slim-fitting, and off-the-shoulder or cropped to show off my curves
c) Chunky, oversize, or cable-knit, in natural colors
d) Black, with a few holes here and there

5. In my room, I have
a) An old-fashioned bed, family pictures in little frames, and girly wallpaper
b) A bed piled with bright pillows, photo collages of my friends, a shag rug, and a funky chair
c) Some shells I found on a beach vacation, a project I made in arts & crafts class, homemade curtains and a painting I found in a flea market
d) Framed album covers or posters, pictures of my favorite bands, shelves stocked with books and magazines I love.

6. When I get the remote, I turn the channel to
a) Any movie with Julia Roberts
b) The funny cartoon everyone at school talks about, or a *Friends* rerun
c) Animal Planet or the Discovery Channel
d) MTV2

7. My screen saver is a picture of
a) My pet, my family, or a sentimental picture
b) Me and my friends hanging out
c) A funky nature scene, or my favorite quote or song lyric
d) The cute lead singer of my current favorite band, CD cover art, or the coolest option my software program offered in a bold color

8. When I read for fun, I usually
a) Pick up a classic love story or a romance novel
b) Flip through magazines or read a chick-lit book with a fun plot and a cute cover
c) Scan the newspaper or check out a classic book at the library from my English class suggested-reading list
d) Prefer mysteries, thrillers, or dark comedies or read blogs online

Your score . . .

If your answers were mostly A's...

You're a die-hard romantic with a sentimental side, and floral patterns of all shapes and sizes, and vintage-inspired prints from the '40s and '50s are very appealing to you. Classic tailored stripes and embroidered patterns are up your alley, too. If you could raid one celebrity closet, it would be **Kate Bosworth's** for fun prints and patterns with a flirty, feminine side. **Renee Zellweger** also loves lady-like romantic prints and puts a cool, retro spin on them to create her own distinct look.

If your answers were mostly B's...

Trends are where your heart is, and you like any-thing-of-the-moment, cute, and fun. Bold patterns that get you noticed—like butterflies, cherries, or flowers—are what you love. In whose closet would you absolutely live if you could? That would have to be **Nicole Richie's,** for patterns that say you're both fash-ionable and feminine.

If your answers were mostly C's...

Natural and grounded are words you would use to describe yourself, so you may like cotton tunics and flowing skirts with ethnic prints imported from places like Bali or India. Small prints such as pais-ley fit with your earthy style too. Even the occasional tie-dye or lace detail may appeal to you. **Vanessa Carlton, Joss Stone**, and **Natasha Bedingfield** all have wardobes you covet.

If your answers were mostly D's...

Bold, tomboyish patterns, like plaids on flannel or western shirts, or vertical striped, skinny pants are what you're into. Because of your rebellious, cool sensibility, anything too girly, like flowers, would feel wrong. Graphic pat-terns—graffiti prints and checkerboard patterns, wide stripes, or band logos—are your thing. **Kelly Clarkson, Fergie**, and **Hilarie Burton** share your style sensibility.

How to pair prints without looking like you got dressed in the dark.

- When it comes to mixing prints and patterns, the general rule is that bold designs don't like competition. A big floral-print top works best with a solid bottom, or just on its own, like in the form of a dress.

A pattern resembling mismatched pendants gives Ashlee Simpson's look its edge.

- Smaller prints, on the other hand, such as pinstripes, small paisleys, small circles, small squares, and tiny flowers, can get along with other small prints very nicely.

A floral gown with a wide sash in a tie-dyed print helps Jessica Simpson make a big entrance.

- Mix tone-on-tone patterns. Say you have a light green shirt with a circle pattern. Put that on under a dark green cardigan sweater that has embroidery or beading. Or try pairing a shirt with blue rugby stripes with a bandanna-print headband in a different shade of blue, or light pink gingham check with a darker pink. Get the idea?

- Pay attention to the scale of a pattern: Are the two prints you're trying to pair exactly the same size? That probably won't work.

Instead, try wearing one piece in a print that is slightly bigger than the print on the other one, like a camisole in a medium-sized floral with summery striped seersucker pants.

- Pair a geometric pattern (stripe or shape) with a natural pattern (flower or plant), for example, an argyle sweater with the collar and cuffs of a tiny-floral shirt peeking out. Or pull a sporty striped sailor sweater over a summery floral dress with a pair of flats or sneakers.

- Try not to mix more than two patterns at a time. Of course, if you're completely confident of your choices, go for it! But when in doubt, simpler is usually better.

SO OUTRAGEOUS IT WORKS

Now that you know the "rules," feel free to break them. Attention-getters like the Queen of Unconventional Style, **Gwen Stefani,** take pattern-mixing to the extreme and couldn't care less if the fashion police have issued a warrant for their arrest.

Gwen Stefani, known for her flair for mixing and matching patterns, bravely pairs plaid with paisley and leopard print.

WHAT COLOR IS RIGHT FOR YOU?

Before we get started on specific colors, we need to explain a color concept that's subtle but really important to understanding how different shades work in relation to one another: the undertone. The "undertone" is the pale or underlying hue of a shade, usually described as "cool" or "warm." Our own coloring—skin tone and eye and hair color—can be described as cool or warm, too.

SKIN TONE

To determine whether your own coloring is cool or warm, consider your natural skin color.

- Does your skin turn a little golden and brown in the summer? Is it caramel-tan all year round? If so, you have warm undertones. If your hair is red, golden brown, chestnut, or honey blonde, you're warm.

- Do you have pale skin that flushes pink when you exercise? Do you have blue eyes and jet-black, pale ashy brown, or very light blonde hair? You have a cool undertone, in that case.

- Many of us fall somewhere in the middle, which is where things can get tricky. But here's the good news: If you are somewhere in the middle, then you're probably pretty neutral and can wear both kinds of colors, if you want. It just depends on which you like more!

WARM HAIR/SKIN/EYES COMBINATIONS

If you have deep brown eyes, dark brown hair, and coffee-colored skin like **KELLY ROWLAND,** you're warm and look best in peach, orange, red, gold, turquoise blue, or brown.

If you have hazel eyes, honey-brown skin and golden brown hair like **RIHANNA,** you're warm, too, so look for colors in the same family.

If you have brown eyes, golden skin and brown hair highlighted blonde like **JESSICA ALBA,** you're warm. Don't let blonde hair fool you. If it's a deep, warm blonde like honey or sun-kissed with streaks, it's warm.

COOL HAIR/SKIN/EYES COMBINATIONS

If you have fair skin, light brown hair and ice-blue eyes like MICHELLE TRACHTENBERG, you're cool and would look best in deep blues, violets, or silvery gray.

If you have very fair skin, pale blonde hair, and blue-green eyes like KIRSTEN DUNST, you're cool.

If you have peachy-pink skin, dark brown hair, and pale blue eyes like ALEXIS BLEDEL, you're also cool. For a super-dramatic effect, wear black—it makes your light eyes stand out even more.

NEUTRAL HAIR/SKIN/EYES COMBINATIONS:

If you have deep blue eyes, golden tan skin, and golden brown hair like MISCHA BARTON, you're neutral. Your skin and hair are warm, but your eyes are cool like a pool of blue water, so nearly any color will work for you.

If you have warm skin, black hair, and deep brown eyes like LUCY LIU, you may think that warm colors are the way to go. But colors that veer to the cool side, like gray or plum, are often your best shades.

UNDERTONES
REVEALED

Just because you have a cool undertone doesn't mean that you can't ever buy a red shirt again! There are warm and cool versions of red, orange, green, blue, purple—you name it. You just have to find one that works.

COOL   **WARM**

Red can be a blue-based **cherry** or a more yellow-toned **fire-engine** hue.

Purple can be a soft bluish **violet,** like the color of the flower, or a warm **plum.**

Blue can be a rich true-blue **cobalt** or a deep yellow-toned **azure,** like the color of the ocean.

Forest green has strong blue undertones; **lime green** has more yellow in it.

Orange can range from a nearly-pink **terra cotta** with blue undertones to a **marigold** with lots of yellow in it.

Whether it's **pearl** or more of a **putty** color, there is a shade of grey for every skin tone.

A blue undertone makes dark **chocolate brown,** while a yellow undertone leans more toward a **coffee** shade.

WARM COLORS

- Any color that looks hot like a flame—brick red, orange, or yellow—or earthy shades like rosy pink, moss green, or bark brown: All of these have warm undertones.

- Warm colors look best on people who have golden, honey-blonde, auburn, chestnut brown, or red hair and light brown, hazel, or green eyes.

- Emma Roberts, Halle Berry, Emmy Rossum, Keira Knightley, and Claire Danes look best in colors with warm undertones.

- You can tell that a color is warm if it looks better when you match it with off-white and brown than pure white and black.

Emma Roberts

Halle Berry

Claire Danes

Keira Knightley

Emmy Rossum

COOL COLORS

- Shades that look cold, more like ice-blue water, a gray winter sky, or like bright petals on flowers—geranium red, violet, sea green—are cool colors.

- Cool colors look best on people who have pale to ash blonde, light brown, or black hair and blue or dark, dark brown eyes.

- Jennifer Garner, Ginnifer Goodwin, Jessica Simpson, and Alicia Keys look better in cool colors.

- You can tell that a color is cool if it looks better when you match it with pure white and black than off-white and brown.

Jennifer Garner

Ginnifer Goodwin

Jessica Simpson

Alicia Keys

There are two BIG buts…there are many people who don't fit so neatly into one category. **Amanda Peet** has cool blue eyes, warm brown hair, and olive-y skin. **Nicole Richie** has pale blue eyes, golden high-lighted hair, and caramel skin. If you're like this too, that just means that both types of shades look good on you, and it's up to you to make the choice. AND just about any color has a shade that's right for you. Now that you're aware that it's not just "a single-color thing," try various shades of the colors you like until you figure out which ones work for you.

THE FASHION ZODIAC

Let your sign show you the way to your new favorite shade

CAPRICORN

Vanessa Paradis

AQUARIUS

Shakira

PISCES

Arielle Kebbel

ARIES

Reese Witherspoon

CAPRICORN 12/22-1/19 Capricorns need colors that are as serious, grounded, and focused as they are, and forest green, gray, and dark brown do the trick.

AQUARIUS 1/20-2/18 Violet and cerulean blue (think of the color of a cloudless sky) appeal to Aquarians, who have a strong-minded, serious side as well as a quirky sensibility. These colors are just as unique and lively as you are.

PISCES 2/19-3/20 Creative, dreamy fish are into fashion, especially

imaginative, romantic, girlish clothes in colors like sea green and powder blue.

ARIES 3/21-4/19 You're a true original, which is why you lean toward red, yellow, and salmon. They appeal to your fiery, risk-taking side and your energy and enthusiasm. You also have a glamorous, impulsive side that isn't afraid to call attention your way.

TAURUS 4/20-5/20 Green is a head-turning color, but in shades like pistachio, kiwi, and emerald, it's still pretty safe. Green

represents the finer things in life, but also has a practical side (both very important to Taurans). A necklace of jade beads is your perfect accessory.

GEMINI 5/21-6/20 Try a mix of colors— especially orange, yellow, and magenta. These colors fit your bubbly personality, your love of trends (tangerine always seems fresh), and dreams of travel, since they're popular shades for fun ethnic jewelry and clothes.

CANCER 6/21-7/22 Cancer crabs are ruled by the moon, so shades

inspired by *la lune* are ideal. Lavender, pearl, ivory, charcoal, and silver can look as romantic and dreamy as you feel. Cancers also like to feel comfortable, and these soothing colors are as easy as it gets.

LEO 7/23-8/22 No sign loves attracting light and attention like Leo, so sparkling gold (especially wearable as an accessory, like shoes, belts, or jewelry) should do the trick. Never shy or retiring, you won't mind turning it up with royal blue or a powerful red, also excellent colors for Leo lions.

TAURUS

Rosario Dawson

GEMINI

Rachel Leigh Cook

CANCER

Lindsay Lohan

LEO

Madonna

VIRGO 8/23-9/22

Virgos like things that are simple and straightforward. What colors could be more fitting than navy blue and shades of brown? Browns appeal to your down-to-earth personality; navy appeals to your preference for simplicity.

LIBRA 9/23-10/22

You're strong (and a little bossy sometimes) and also quite charming and social, so you need a color that is both sweet and assertive. Try pink (especially fuchsia or raspberry) or blue (like a pale sea foam or a rich azure).

SCORPIO 10/23-11/21

Your intense, focused personality calls for the most dramatic color: black. You like to feel mysterious and play off your natural magnetism, and a sexy black dress is the ideal choice (if you're feeling extra daring, make it in leather!).

SAGITTARIUS 11/22-12/21

Your sporty, optimistic side will love royal blue and purple—maybe in a hooded sweatshirt or a cable-knit sweater. These colors are as bright, creative, and up for a new adventure as you are.

VIRGO

Hilary Duff

LIBRA

Rachel McAdams

SCORPIO

Kelly Osbourne

SAGITTARIUS

Jojo

65

4 JEANS, +

T-SHIRT SNEAKER

Essentials

JEANS, T-SHIRT + SNEAKER ESSENTIALS

We know, we know! You wear these three items practically every single day. But if you keep experimenting with new shapes and styles, you'll never get stuck in a jeans and T-shirt rut. There's a pair of jeans that will flatter every figure, a comfortable T-shirt for every day of the week, and a pair of sneakers that works with just about any outfit, so the possible combinations are endless, but some universal rules apply:

- Ignore size in favor of fit. Sizes vary from brand to brand. If you have to buy one size bigger or smaller than you usually wear, who cares? What's important is that it fits and flatters your body.

- When it comes to showing skin, don't go overboard—cropped T-shirts that expose your belly are so 1999! Seriously, jeans that expose your undies and T-shirts that expose your midriff aren't very polished, or stylish, for that matter. If you want to show some skin, try showing off your shoulders or collarbone. It's much more subtle and sophisticated.

- Consider the shrinkage factor when you're buying cotton clothes. If a T-shirt is super-tight when you try it on in the store, how's it going to fit once you wash it? Tissue-thin cotton T-shirts need to be hand-washed and hung to dry in order to keep their shape and size. You may want to buy a size up just in case.

- Attention, compulsive sneaker shoppers: Control yourself! Fergie may have 50 pairs lined up in her closet, but that doesn't mean you have to!

Amerie dresses up her jeans with a sweet lace jacket.

EVERYTHING YOU NEED TO KNOW ABOUT . . .
JEANS

Sometimes it seems as if there are more jeans in the world than people to wear them. How can you possibly sort through all of those styles and find a pair that looks like it was built for you? It's not as hard as it seems. You just need a little patience (to try on a bunch and see which fits best) and a little information.

1. KEEP IN MIND YOUR BODY TYPE.

Each body type—tall, petite, curvy, lean—looks best in a particular fit. For example, no matter how trendy stovepipe (super-tapered) jeans may be, they may not be a good choice if you want to take the emphasis off of your curvy hips. Because they're fitted at the bottom, they call attention to the width difference between your hips and your ankles. Instead, try a pair that flare out slightly from the knee down to make your legs look more even. If you're short, jeans that drag behind your shoes will weigh you down and you'll look like you're wearing pants that are too big for your tiny frame (which you are).

2. CONSIDER THE RISE.

It's a word you hear all of the time when jeans shopping, but what is it, really? It's the measurement of the seam from the crotch to the waistband. Check out the length of the zipper as an easy way to determine what the rise is. If it's really short, it's low-rise, which means more of your middle (and if you're curvy, your bum) will show. If it's really long, the waist will hit high, near your belly button. If you feel narrow and want to appear curvier, this is a good choice. Otherwise, steer clear. Most of us look best in a medium-low rise that hits just below the belly button.

3. TAKE A CLOSE LOOK AT THE POCKETS.

Check out "Pocket Size and Shape" on page 73 to see what the right angle, positioning, and width of a pocket can do to help you in that area!

4. FOR THE MOST FLATTERING LOOK, BUY JEANS THAT FIT.

It's tempting to slouch around in old jeans that drag on the ground. Even if you usually wear loose pants, try to find jeans that fit on the snug side. Otherwise, they'll sag and droop in the butt, and that doesn't flatter anyone's curves.

5. CONSIDER WHAT SHOES YOU'LL WEAR WITH THEM.

Your jeans should fall about ¼ to ½ of an inch above the floor in the back, by the heel of your shoe. That means you might need one pair of jeans to wear with sneakers and one that you wear with taller shoes.

CROPPED JEANS

Cropped jeans are cut below the knee but above the ankle and aren't tight around the calves. For shoes, wear sandals, flats, or low heels to show skin around the ankle and make legs look their longest, since cropped jeans can make legs appear shorter. They can also be a good choice with narrow, high-heeled boots for a long, lean look.

BEWARE OF CROPPED JEANS IF...

- You're petite, since they can make legs look smaller than they are.

- You're long-waisted, since they can make legs look shorter and out of proportion to your torso.

- You're wearing socks and sneakers. We repeat, do NOT wear cropped jeans with socks and sneakers! It will make your legs look dramatically shorter. Trust us.

- You have thicker calves and ankles you'd rather not show off.

BOOT-CUT

This is the most universally flattering cut for all body types, since they are fitted through the thighs and flare out slightly from the knee to the ankle, making the leg look longer and proportional. Sure, you can wear them with boots, but they're good with any shoe. Make sure the rise is low (a couple of inches below the belly button is most flattering for everyone) and they're long enough to cover most of the back of your shoes.

BEWARE OF BOOT-CUT JEANS IF...

- The fit is too tight. If boot-cut jeans are too snug, they can make your thighs look larger than they are.

BOYFRIEND JEANS

It's no surprise that boyfriend jeans are jeans that look like you borrowed them from a guy, right? They're slightly baggy, and may be slightly shredded or worn in, too. Every once in a while, it feels great to put on a pair of loose jeans and just hang out. With a T-shirt and flip-flops or flat sandals in the summer, or a favorite old sweater when it's cooler, it's the most relaxed look you can get.

BEWARE OF BOYFRIEND JEANS IF...

- You're dressing up. It's a slacker look that's better for daytime.

- You're concerned about looking slouchy or heavier than you are. Too-big, loose jeans don't make you look smaller. The opposite is true! Wear snugger fitting jeans for a more flattering fit.

FLARED

Like the boot-cut jean, flares taper out from the knee down. The difference is that flares are wider at the hem. Also known as bell bottoms, they create a dramatic, mermaid-curvy shape on your lower half. If you're narrow on the bottom and like that retrolook, this is a fun cut to experiment with.

BEWARE OF FLARED JEANS IF...

- You're petite. The heaviness at the hem will drag you into the ground.

- You're curvy on the bottom, and don't want to call attention to it.

- You're long-waisted, because flares can make legs look shorter and out of proportion to your torso.

TAPERED

Jeans that become more fitted from the hip to the ankle are tapered. They'll make a narrow frame appear curvier, and are a good choice to pair with an oversize jacket or sweater to keep the proportions right (Baggy tops look best with snug-fitting bottoms, and vice-versa.) Look for a pair with a lower rise, since high-waisted tapered jeans can look old-fashioned and retro (in a bad way).

BEWARE OF TAPERED JEANS IF...
- You're curvy on the bottom, because the taper will call attention to the width difference between broader hips and tiny ankles.
- You have thicker calves and ankles, since they may be too snug at the bottom.

STOVEPIPE

Popular with wiry rock stars and models, stove pipe jeans are straight-up-and-down (like a pipe—hence the name). Their straight, narrow shape makes them a cute match for a blousy top. Shorter girls with petite frames will love them for making their legs look longer. This cut is perfect for boyish, narrow bodies, but if you have major curves on the bottom, they're not the best choice.

BEWARE OF STOVEPIPE JEANS IF...
- You're curvy on the bottom. This straight-up-and-down style doesn't make room for a womanly shape.

WIDE-LEG

Jeans with wide-cut legs fit more like pants than most denim does. It's a slightly dressier look, kind of like sailors' pants, especially if they fasten at the waistband like dress pants do. With a snug T-shirt, sleeveless blouse or tank top in summer, cropped jackets or a slim-fitting turtleneck in winter (to balance out the baggier proportion on the bottom) they can be a smart and stylish look.

BEWARE OF WIDE-LEG JEANS IF...
- You're short. The wideness on your bottom half will make your legs look shorter.
- You're curvy on top, and aren't comfortable wearing snug-fitting shirts. You'll need to wear something fitted on the top to get the proportions right.

CAPRI

Like cropped jeans, capris fall somewhere between the knee and the ankle. The difference is that capris are a little more narrow, and fit snugly around the thighs and calves. They're cute in the summer with a delicate blouse or a tee and sandals, or in the winter with an oversize sweater and girlish shoes or tucked into boots (you don't have extra fabric to stuff in there). Make sure they're snug, but not too tight, for the most flattering look.

BEWARE OF CAPRI JEANS IF...
- You're curvy on the bottom. The narrow legs can call attention to broader hips.
- You have thicker calves and ankles you'd rather not show off.

WASHES

There's a reason why people don't call denim "blue jeans" anymore. There are so many shades of blue and different treatments for the fabric that just one word isn't descriptive enough.

DARK-WASH

This is the deepest shade of blue that jeans can get. It's great for everyday jeans that can also be upgraded to nighttime and going out, since they're the dressiest, most sophisticated wash.

SANDBLASTED

Jeans are (you guessed it!) blasted with sand to give them a worn-in, casual look that would take years to create on your own. The lightest part is usually on the tops of the thighs, which can make legs look thinner (white makes things stand out, and dark shadows make things less noticeable, so the contrast makes the thighs look smaller).

FADED

If jeans are light blue all over, not just in specific patches, they're faded. It can be hard to match colors with faded denim: They're so light that they don't look great with black, dark brown, or earthy neutrals. Save the faded wash for an extra pair, not for the pair you depend on every day.

VINTAGE (OR ANTIQUE)

An antique wash is a deep blue, somewhere between faded and dark wash. It looks a little worn in, but naturally so, not sandblasted or frayed. This is also a great wash for daytime, but requires a little more effort to dress up at night.

PRE-WORN OR "DESTROYED"

A lot of brands like to make their jeans look like they were dragged behind a car for 4 miles or worn by a mechanic for a few months. They're definitely not for dress-up, and sometimes, the "distressed" look (like big holes in the knees) can get out of control. This look is for really casual days, or to wear when you feel rebellious. Why not wait until your old jeans get wrecked on their own, and help them along with scissors, instead of spending the extra money for someone else to do it?

Kelly Osbourne prefers destroyed jeans. Is anyone surprised by this?

WHISKERS

The little white, worn creases from the zipper placket out toward the hips are known as whiskers. They can make jeans look worn in, and be flattering to your curves. Once again, they can look overdone, so the subtler the better.

POCKET SIZE AND SHAPE: WHICH IS THE MOST FLATTERING?

Even if you're in love with the cut and wash, the wrong back pockets can make a good pair of jeans look bad faster than you can say "Levi's."

- Large pockets can make hips appear wider; so will pockets that are set too close to the side seams.

- Small, high pockets tend to make bums look bigger and rounder. If that's what you want, great! If not, stay away.

- With asymmetrical pockets, if the inner side (closest to the center seam) is shorter than the outer side (closest to your hip), it will give your backside a little lift.

- Flap pockets are good for a flat fanny, but they are the enemy of anyone who doesn't want to make their bottom look bigger.

- Any body type will look best in jeans that have pockets that are centered and in proportion to the pant. And remember, the bigger the design and stitching on the pocket, the more attention you'll draw to it. So keep it simple if you don't want to show it off.

- Any pocket too low will make even the perkiest backside seem saggy. Look for pockets that sit in the middle of the bum.

24-HOUR JEANS
FOR ALL SEASONS!

In style with everything from a girly camisole to your favorite comfy T-shirt, jeans just might be a more versatile wardrobe staple than you think.

JEANS FOR DAY...IN THE SPRING AND SUMMER

• With a fitted T-shirt or tank top, flat sandals, a leather belt and a bag, jeans look instantly laid-back and cool.

• With a silky camisole under a cardigan, jeans are a casual but slightly feminine look perfect for school or the beach.

• Light-colored denim with a colorful halter top or a sheer printed shirt (over a tank top, of course) is a neat and pretty look for warm weather.

Michelle Trachtenberg

JEANS FOR DAY...IN THE FALL AND WINTER

• When the temperature drops, add a pair of boots and a chunky sweater for a cozy, bohemian look.

• With a cable-knit sweater and a fitted jacket, jeans make even the preppiest prepster look pulled together and chic.

• Pair jeans with a T-shirt and a leather jacket and boots for a classic, slightly rebellious look. Don't put away your cropped jeans

when summer ends! This look is especially cute when you can expose lots of boot under short jeans.

JEANS FOR NIGHT...IN THE FALL AND WINTER

• Throw a velvet jacket over a silky shirt for an elegant cooler-weather look. Try

America Fererra

Jessica Biel

Christina Ricci

Sophie Okonedo

wearing open-toe sandals or sling-backs with fun knee-high stockings (in bold colors or fishnet) to add another dressy detail.

• Give denim a nighttime edge with big, bold accessories like long, sequined scarves, rhinestone brooches on your jacket, or over-the-top jewelry.

• A sequined or beaded sweater worn with jeans and boots is dressy enough to wear out at night. Try an oversize sweater with a belt, and tuck your jeans into your boots for a rock-and-roll touch.

JEANS FOR NIGHT...IN THE SPRING AND SUMMER

• Dressing up denim is easy, especially in summer. Just add something feminine or unexpected.

• A sparkly belt, decorated with rhinestones or made of chain, is an instant dressy touch to take jeans from day to night. Wear sandals that match the color of the metal (silver or gold) for an extra-fancy touch.

• Nothing dresses up jeans and a T-shirt quite like colorful heels and bright lipstick. Keep it super simple with white T-shirt, a ponytail, and a clean face; this is always a pretty—and easy—nighttime look for summer.

Jojo

Pamela Anderson

Kristin Cavalleri

D.I.Y. JEAN GENIUS

There are jeans. And then there are your extra, double-favorite jeans that have worn in just the right way. One easy way to make a pair your own is to customize your denim for one-of-a-kind looks you won't see anywhere else. Here are some easy ideas to try at home.

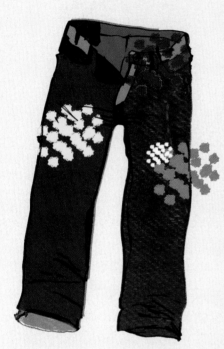

FABRIC PAINT

Using brushes, stamps, or sponges loaded up with paint, get creative. Since you have so much control over where the paint goes and how much you'll use, you can use many colors to paint complicated pictures and patterns or write a favorite quote. NOTE: Use only paint designed for fabric so it doesn't come off in the wash!

SPRAY PAINT

Holding the can 10 inches away, spray shapes or bursts of color onto the jeans. Pick a single design (like letters, circles, big dots of various sizes) using several colors, or use just one color and experiment with the shapes.

STENCIL

Cut letters or shapes out of heavy card stock or cardboard. Or buy stencils at an art or office supply store. Tape the stencil into position (wherever you want to paint the design) and either use spray paint or apply a light layer of fabric paint. Find cool-looking letters in old books or on the computer and stencil your initials onto the back pocket for a subtle way to personalize your pants.

PATCHES ON THE OUTSIDE

You don't need a hole to apply a patch! Buy colorful patches from your local fabric or craft-stores or head to the record store to find badges from your favorite band. Use just one, a few similar small ones, or collect a bunch and sew them on in a cluster for a real punk-rock look.

PATCHES FROM THE INSIDE

Take an old shirt or a fabric remnant and cut a patch that's about an inch bigger than the hole in your jeans on all sides. Turn your jeans inside out, apply a line of fabric glue about a half inch away from the edge, and then place the fabric on top with the back facing you. Seal the edges, let dry, and when you turn the jeans right side out, you'll have a patch and the cute frayed look. You can also do it by hand with a needle and thread. Use a running stitch (pass the needle in and out of the fabric evenly) in contrasting colors to turn an accidental hole into a style statement.

FOR IRON-ONS

Heat up the iron. Put the patch where you want it. Hold the iron on top of the patch until the heat melts the glue on the back and the patch sticks to the denim (sometimes instructions recommend putting a light layer of fabric, like a pillow case, between the iron and the patch to keep it from burning).

FOR SEW-ONS

Put the patch where you want it. Thread a needle, tie off the end, and start by bringing the needle through the jeans from the inside out (so that you won't see the knot). Make diagonal stitches over the edge of the patch, spacing them evenly. End the last stitch on the wrong side and tie the ends of the thread off.

BEADS

Add a little razzle-dazzle to regular old jeans with beads. All shapes and sizes can be used to outline pockets, make random daisies, or make your monogram. Thread a needle, tie off the end, and start by bringing the needle through the jeans from the inside out (so you won't see the knot). Load on one bead or a few, push the needle back through the denim, then back up to the front, and repeat with more beads until you've finished your design. Push the needle back through to the wrong side and tie the ends of the thread off.

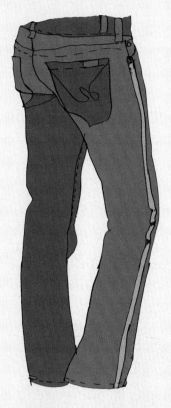

RIBBON

Find your favorite color, plaid, gingham, or preppy stripe ribbon and sew or glue it along the vertical seams of the jeans on the outside of the leg, or along the hem at the bottom of each leg. And if you sew or glue black ribbon down the outside seams of black jeans, you've got everyday tuxedo pants!

TIP: You can get crafty even if you don't have a sewing machine. Fabric glue, a hot glue gun, and no-sew iron-on hem tape are quick fixes when you're looking to have some fun with your favorite old clothes.

EVERYTHING YOU NEED TO KNOW ABOUT . . .
T-SHIRTS

Can you ever have enough T-shirts? Yes and no. Since it's the item you probably wear the most, you may be tempted to pick up a new one every time you're shopping—your budget might say otherwise! Get the essentials, and then add more fun ones only when you've got the extra cash.

- Basic white and black T-shirts with short and long sleeves are always good investments. Worn on their own or as a layering piece, you'll get a lot of mileage out of them.
- A few flattering tank tops in fun colors are also layering staples. Find some with built-in bras if you don't need extra support on top and wear them on their own, or under just about anything.
- A couple of "dress-up" T-shirts—with fun ties, gathers, designs, even beading—are an easy way to express your style.

CREWNECK

A crewneck comes all the way up and covers your collarbone. Make sure it's not too snug around your neck, or too loose. A T-shirt with a bulky band around the neckline has an athletic, boyish look. Find crewnecks that have flatter bands and hit slightly below the collarbone.

BEWARE OF A CREWNECK IF...
- You're curvy on top. A high neck can exaggerate your chest, especially if it's a stretchy or fitted T-shirt. Try a slightly lower neck and a cotton fabric that doesn't cling to your shape.

V-NECK

You guessed it—a V-neck dips down to a V in front. It's a very feminine look that can show off your curves, and your necklace if you're a jewelry fan. V-necks can also minimize broader shoulders and help to create the look of curves on top.

BEWARE OF A V-NECK IF...
- You're curvy on top and don't want to show it off.

BOATNECK

A wide neck that opens out toward the collarbone is a boatneck (when you look at the T-shirt when it's laying flat, the neck looks kind of like the bottom of a boat). This is a flattering style for just about any body type.

BEWARE OF A BOATNECK IF...
- You have very broad shoulders, because the neck is cut horizontally and can emphasize width in this area.

SCOOP NECK

On a scoop neck, the neckline dips down to expose some of your breastbone and chest. This very feminine look is great if you like to wear beaded necklaces and scarves, since it exposes more skin up top. An open scoop neck can also balance out broader hips, because it makes shoulders look a little wider. A gently scooped neck that's not too low is a good choice if you're curvy on top, too—it creates a smooth line and won't expose cleavage.

BEWARE OF A SCOOP NECK IF...

- It's too large, because it may droop open when you bend over.
- You have very broad shoulders and bigger upper arms, because it may make them appear larger.

HENLEY

A henley has a button-up placket in the front at the neckline. It's styled after an old-fashioned man's undershirt and makes an excellent layering piece, and it can be flattering for all body shapes. Pair with a lower rise, since high-waisted tapered jeans can look retro in a bad way.

BEWARE OF A HENLEY IF...

- You're curvy on top, because the buttons could pull a little. A slightly larger size may solve that problem.

BOYS

Boys' T-shirts have thicker and wider neckbands, and the shoulders are a little squarer and broader. These shirts are fun to throw on over a long-sleeve T-shirt for a slightly tomboyish look, or to wear when you're playing sports or bumming around the house.

BEWARE OF A BOYS T-SHIRT IF...

- You're interested in wearing flattering tees that skim along your curves.

Find the right fit!

When it comes to buying T-shirts you'll love, the right fit is crucial—even more important than color and cut.

- A T-shirt that's too tight can reveal everything underneath it, like bra straps, bulges, belly buttons, and more. Make sure the fit is snug, but not restrictive.

- Choose tank tops with a built-in bra or wide straps to avoid multiple-strap syndrome.

- Short sleeves can also be tricky. A cap sleeve is the most flattering; it makes your arms and waist look trimmer. Boxy sleeves can add extra bulk, and may be better off in your gym locker, or worn during practice or washing the car!

- T-shirts that hit at the waistband of your jeans or below are the most flattering for every body. Any tee that reveals too much of your entire lower back when you bend over is probably too short for you.

A SLEEVE-LENGTH PRIMER

CAMISOLE
No sleeves, just thin straps like bra straps

TANK TOP
Has no sleeves, straps wider than camisole straps

SLEEVELESS
Ends at the shoulder

CAP SLEEVES
Juts out slightly past the shoulder in a short, diagonally cut sleeve

SHORT SLEEVE
Falls mid-way between the shoulder and the elbow

THREE-QUARTER LENGTH
Hits just below the elbow, or at the mid-point between the elbow and the wrist

BELL SLEEVE
Gets bigger toward the wrist and fans out in a bell shape

LONG SLEEVE
Hits at the wrist or slightly longer.

Common T-shirt fabric

RIBBED COTTON It has tiny grooves that give it a slightly rough, textured feeling. The ribs give the fabric a little more stretch.

WHISPER-WEIGHT Lighter than regular cotton T-shirts and designed for layering without extra bulk, whisper-weight (sometimes called tissue) tees can be see-through and look better if you wear two at a time (a tank top under short sleeves, for example).

STRETCH COTTON This is cotton with a little spandex or elastic woven into it to give it a snugger fit. For the most flattering fit, make sure it's large enough not to cling to every curve or expose the workings of your bra.

COTTON-POLYESTER BLEND The added synthetic fibers keep cotton from shrinking and fading but may not be as soft or pleasant to the touch.

T-SHIRTS
FOR DAY OR NIGHT

Everybody's favorite wardrobe staple, a T-shirt can be worn in dozens of ways. Worn alone or as a layering piece, they are a 12-months-a-year basic, regardless of your style or body type.

Nicky Hilton

Mischa Barton

T-SHIRTS FOR DAY...IN THE FALL AND WINTER

- As a layering piece, T-shirts keep wool sweaters from itching and add a shot of color to your winter wardrobe.
- Under a fitted corduroy or wool jacket, a tee adds an extra layer of warmth...and style.
- A short-sleeve T-shirt thrown on over a long-sleeve T-shirt is a boyish, cool, slightly retro look.

Sophia Bush

Jewel

T-SHIRTS FOR DAY...IN THE SPRING AND SUMMER

- With a lightweight cotton skirt and sandals, T-shirts look perfectly ladylike in warm weather.
- T-shirts with denim minis and flip-flops are great for lazy summer days.
- Pair a tee with dressier jeans, flats or sandals, and a colorful belt, and you're ready for school or a day out with your friends.

Mischa Barton

T-SHIRTS FOR NIGHT…IN THE SPRING AND SUMMER

- Find a great pair of dangly earrings and some fun flats, and your basic T-shirt is ready for a night out.
- Slip on a T-shirt or tank with a beaded, brocade, or sequined skirt for a grown-up and effortless look.
- Paired with white jeans or summery cotton pants and a pair of sandals, a T-shirt's ready for any special event.

Amanda Bynes

Amanda Peet

T-SHIRTS FOR NIGHT…IN THE FALL AND WINTER

- With a velvet or faux-fur jacket, some red lipstick, and dark denim jeans, a T-shirt can even be red-carpet ready.
- Wear a T-shirt and layers of necklaces, or wrap a long scarf around your neck a few times for a bohemian take on nighttime dressing.
- Under a stylish shrug or oversized sweater, a tee is an essential layering piece.

DIY T-SHIRT TRICKERY!

It's your old T-shirt's lucky day! Here are 7 ways to give it a second chance.

1 A tee that's too small or faded to wear on its own makes a great layering piece. Thinner tees or camisoles can look so stylish when you pile one on top of another. Choose two shirts in coordinating colors and let the first layer peek out at the bottom.

2 Cut off the sleeves and make it a cute tank top. Give it a slightly military look by sewing patches on the front and bunching the shoulders together and securing them with a gold or silver chain from the crafts store.

3 Change the color! Channel your inner hippie and break out the tie-dye. Or just dye it a few shades darker. This works even with old concert tees, or anything with writing on it.

4 Sew buttons of various sizes along the neckline for a necklace effect. Pick out buttons in coordinating colors or fun shapes, or for a slightly dressier look, try metal buttons with a silver or gold finish.

5 Take a T-shirt that's slightly baggy at the waistline and cut four 2-inch vertical slits in the front and in the back, lace it with a ribbon and tie it as a belt.

6 Cut some small slits or holes into a shirt that can be layered over another tee or a tank top, letting the color of the undershirt show through a bit.

7 Try tracing a favorite design onto an old white T-shirt as a fun art project. (What's the worst that could happen? You'd throw it away, which you were about to do anyway!) With computer transfer paper (available at office-supply stores), you can print out your own pictures or sayings. You could even print out an inside joke that only a few friends know, and watch them crack up when they see you wearing it.

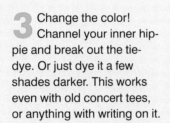

EVERYTHING YOU NEED TO KNOW ABOUT . . .
SNEAKERS

TRAINERS Gym shoes with colorful stripes and logos on them, these are comfortable shoes that are perfect for sports and activities, but are pretty hard to dress up to look cute.

HIGH-TOPS Basketball high-tops, wrestling shoes, or old-school canvas high-tops can make a fun fashion statement.

CASUAL Casual sneakers are not made for sports, but they make great, basic everyday shoes to wear with jeans, shorts, even the occasional dress!

OLD-SCHOOL Sneakers from the '60s and '70s have made a serious comeback. They can be rock and roll, preppy, or a little bohemian, depending on the outfit, and are an inexpensive style staple.

HIGH-TECH With reflective materials and mesh or net on the outside, sneaker companies get really creative making the lightest, most comfortable shoes possible. These can be fun style statements for anybody who has to have the latest, of-the-moment item.

SLIP-ONS Skater shoes first hit it big in the late 1970s and never went away. A little punk, always cool, it's a fun, free-spirited shoe for every day.

COLLECTORS' ITEMS These limited edition styles are worth hundreds of dollars, making them more than a little impractical for every day!

M.I.A. wears lace-free Converse—a fun twist on an old standby.

Sneakers to prom? Stranger things have happened . . .

Lindsay Lohan

The rapper M.I.A. pretty much lives in hers. When Lindsay Lohan hiked up her ballgown on the set of a recent video, guess what was underneath? Vans! In real life, as in your life, there are five simple rules to follow when it comes to rocking casual kicks in unusual ways.

- If your dress is busy, keep the sneakers simple, but if your outfit is basic, don't be afraid to have fun with patterns or a hi-tech style.

- Look for sneakers in unexpected materials or bright color combinations, like metallics or floral prints. Leave your cross-trainers at the gym.

- Sneakers are especially fun when you wear them with something floor-length. Everyone will be especially surprised when they spy your slip-ons on the dance floor (where you can stay for hours, because your shoes are so comfortable!).

- It may be best to stick to more predictable footwear if the party you're going to will be mostly adults (or if seeing you in your sneaks will make your grandmother cry).

DIY SNEAKER STYLE

Here are 5 fun ways to customize your favorite kicks.

1 Design them yourself. Sneaker Websites like Converse.com, Vans.com, and Nike.com let you create a shoe just for you, in a variety of colors and fabrics, to make your very own one-of-a-kind sneaker. What's cooler than that?

2 Make a statement with laces. Trade in boring white shoelaces for black, pink, green, blue, even multicolored laces. They're only a couple of bucks a pair, so buy a few and change them up to match your outfit. Believe it or not, bowling alleys or bowling supply stores stock laces in unexpected colors. Or try Welovecolors.com or Lacesforless.com for dozens of options.

3 Give stencils a shot. Why not paint hearts, your initials, a dragonfly, stars, even a skull and crossbones your shoes? Arts and crafts supply stores offer all kinds of stencils that make painting designs easy. Use an oil-based or acrylic fabric paint (which will work on leather and suede, too) that won't come off in water so your artwork won't rinse off in the rain. Practice first on a piece of paper until you feel confident that you know how to do it. Pick the spot where you want your design. Then secure the stencil to your shoe with some tape. Dab the paint on with a special stencil applicator or a sponge. Wait for the paint to dry completely and remove the stencil.

4 Break out the spray paint. On canvas or leather sneakers, a little spray paint goes a long way. Spray a stripe diagonally across the front toe and the back heel, or create dots of different sizes. Want to change the color of your shoes entirely? Take out the laces and spray the entire shoe (let the paint dry and add another coat for more intense color). Cover the parts you don't want to paint with masking tape, then take it off once the paint dries. Or you can paint the whole shoe the same color. This looks particularly cool with metallic paint, like gold or silver, with black laces.

5 Doodle around. Sometimes, just a ballpoint pen is all you need to put your signature on your shoes. Pick an old, beat-up pair of canvas kicks to try it out first. Draw dots, squiggles, flowers, stars, any design that you like. You can even write your favorite sayings or song lyrics along the edges. You don't have to cover the whole sneaker right away—make it a work in progress. It could be a fun way to pass the time when you're bored. Think of your sneaks as a walking work of art!

5 UNDER +

COVER
Over-the-top

UNDERCOVER + *Over-the-top*

What's under your clothes (and on top of them) can make or break an outfit.

No getup, no matter how cute or original or perfect, can look and feel great if it's worn with undies that don't fit. Period. Bras and underpants are called "foundation garments" for a reason. Like building a house, when you're getting dressed you always start with a sound foundation.

The same goes for after you're dressed. A coat's function is to keep you warm and dry, but when it's the first (and sometimes only, if you live in a cold place) article of clothing anyone sees on you for several months of the year, it's also a style-defining purchase.

HERE'S WHAT YOU SHOULD KNOW ABOUT THE BEGINNING OF AN OUTFIT...

- Nude or flesh-toned bras may not be the cutest option, but they're the easiest to wear. It's tempting to stock up on clean white cotton bras, or cute ones in bright colors and patterns. But if you wear a lot of T-shirts, a nude bra with a smooth finish is the way to go. It's nearly invisible under almost anything, which is what you're going for.

- Thongs or G-strings aren't the only choices if you want to avoid panty lines. Undies that are thin enough and don't have bulky elastic look smooth under jeans. Look for tissue-thin cotton, nylon, or microfiber bikini bottoms that cover your whole rear (the elastic should hit right about where your bum and your leg meet), and there won't be a line in sight.

- When you're wearing sheer clothes, throw a simple tank top underneath. A tank top with a built-in bra or one with straps wide enough to conceal your bra will give you great coverage under flimsy blouses and tops.

- Stock up on undies if you don't like laundry! You'd be surprised how many days you can go between laundry loads if you have at least 10 pairs of underpants you like.

AND THE END OF AN OUTFIT...

- Invest in one classic, all-purpose coat for winter, like a peacoat or a simple knee-length coat, then build your outerwear wardrobe from there.

- A good raincoat (one that actually keeps the water out) is a must. No one is counting style points in a thunderstorm.

- Change the look of a basic winter coat with accessories, like long striped scarves, mittens, knit hats, furry hats... you name it.

Reese Witherspoon is wearing the ultimate all-purpose coat. Over a dress, like it's shown here, it's subtle and tailored. But it's just as cute and easy over pants or jeans for day.

EVERYTHING YOU NEED TO KNOW ABOUT. . . BRAS

A bra that squeezes your back and creates bulges around its straps, or doesn't offer enough support in the front, can ruin the look of an otherwise amazing T-shirt. Undies can creep up and expose themselves over the waistband of your jeans or pinch your cheeks (the other cheeks) and ruin the line of pants. But these mistakes are easily avoided, if you know how to buy comfortable, well-fitting underwear for your body type and personal style.

WHICH BRAS ARE LIKELY TO WORK FOR YOU:

FOR A CUPS

A smooth-cup underwire bra gives you a boost and is undetectable under fitted tops. Demi-cups give you a boost and support, and push-up bras have a way of creating serious cleavage out of the blue! Triangle-cup bras are an excellent casual choice.

FOR B CUPS

A tiny bit of padding, a smooth cup, and a supportive underwire are all a B-cup girl needs. If you're craving more cleavage, try a clasp-front push-up bra or a demi-cup style. Triangle-cup and soft bras don't offer much support at all for your curves, but if you like the natural look, go for it.

FOR C CUPS

Slightly wider straps help with heavier lifting. Once again, look for bras with the underwire, so you can be sure to get enough support. Racer-back styles offer a little more lift and support. If you don't want to add more bulk but want a smooth look with lots of coverage, look for bras with thin padding.

FOR D CUPS

Look for bras with generous coverage, wide straps, and underwire to get the support you need. That doesn't mean they have to look like grandma's bra, though. Find a style with pretty, lacy straps. Minimizers (bras with cups that offer firm support of your entire chest) are perfect to wear with thin tees or sheer tops.

TRIANGLE BRA

If you're smaller on top, and don't need a ton of support, this is comfortable and easy to fit.

RACER-BACK BRA

The straps meet in the middle of the back. It's designed to be worn with sleeveless shirts or tank tops so the straps won't slip off of your shoulders.

UNDERWIRE BRA

For medium to larger sized curves and a natural shape, try an underwire bra without any padding. The C-shaped curved wire gives support, but it shouldn't be so tight that it leaves a mark in your skin when you take it off.

CONVERTIBLE BRA

Don't waste your money on a straight-up strapless bra for a special-event dress when you can buy one that has removable straps that can be worn crisscross, as a halter or diagonally, anytime you need it.

MOLDED BRA

This shape, which has a form of its own and is slightly thicker, gives you a little more coverage without bulky padding. This is a great option under a thin T-shirt to keep you covered.

DEMI-CUP BRA

Demi means half, so demi cups offer a little less coverage than full-size cup bras. They can boost the curves of a small bust, and look really cute, but they can be too obvious under a T-shirt.

DOUBLE OR THICK STRAP BRA

For a big bust, these larger straps offer much-needed support and don't dig into your shoulders.

PADDED BRA

To fill out your dress a little more, or just for a little extra oomph, try a padded bra. Some styles have removable pads, so you can take them out or adjust them to better support your curves.

MINIMIZER BRA

Similar to a sports bra, minimizers will take the emphasis off of a large bust when you want to contain your curves.

FRONT-CLASP BRA

You guessed it! It clasps in the front. Cleavage-enhancing or push-up bras often come with a front clasp.

EVERYTHING YOU NEED TO KNOW ABOUT. . . UNDIES

Because you can't try them on in the store (and we're sure you wouldn't want to), buying undies is all about trial and error. Pick up a few inexpensive pairs in different styles and experiment to find the right style for you. Make sure you have at least a few pairs without patterns on them in neutral colors for when you wear light-colored clothes. And always buy undies with a cotton crotch for comfort and better circulation.

BOYSHORTS

Comfy to sleep in, and perfect to wear under mini-skirts or dresses (to feel completely covered if the wind blows, or when you're sitting down), boyshorts are the cutest undie style to come along in years.

BRIEFS

Totally functional and practical, briefs are the all-purpose underpant. If the fabric is thin enough, they're not noticeable under skirts or pants, and way more comfortable than thongs—for obvious reasons!

LOWRIDER OR HIPSTER BRIEFS

These are absolutely essential if you wear low-rise pants and jeans. The exposed-thong-strap look is so tacky!

Avoid embarrassing exposure by wearing underpants that hit lower on the hips.

BIKINI

With less coverage than a brief and more than a thong, bikini undies are a good compromise. Make sure the fabric is thin and the elastic doesn't dig into your skin. It's uncomfortable, for one, and likely to show through your pants or jeans if it does.

STRING BIKINI

Unlike regular bikinis, these are held together with thin straps on the sides. They're really about the same other than that, and which type you wear is just a matter of preference.

THONG

With a narrow strip of fabric in the back, thong undies leave your cheeks exposed. They were first made popular by women who wanted to avoid underwear lines, but since they've been around, waistbands have

gotten lower and new problems have arrived. An exposed thong is the cheesiest thing ever, so try to avoid this calamity by wearing low-rise thongs.

MINIMIZERS

On the opposite end of the underwear spectrum are control underpants, designed to suck in your middle for a smoother line under dresses. If you feel like you're bulging out in odd places, these can really help smooth out the bunches. Everybody needs a little help now and then.

UNDERWEAR ISSUES, SOLVED!

1 HOW DO I KEEP MY STRAPLESS BRA FROM SLIPPING?
Buy one that fits, and clasp it on the tightest hooks. Many strapless bras have a slightly sticky strip of elastic at the top that helps keep a bra from sliding off. If you have a strapless dress and are afraid of major slippage, do what many brides do and have a tailor sew bra cups into the bust. They work like a charm.

2 THE TANK TOP DILEMMA: ARE EXPOSED STRAPS A NO-NO?
The answer is: It depends. If you have plain-old flesh-toned or white bra straps, you do not want them to be peeking out from under your tank. If you have thin, pretty bra straps in a fun color, a little bit of exposure might be okay. This is a personal preference. If your style is classic, tailored and neat, it's a no-no. But if you're more free-spirited, the occasional showing of strap is fine. Try not to make it a habit, though, since it can look messy and inappropriate for school.

3 BOY SHORT UNDIES: ARE THEY FIGURE-FLATTERING OR BULK-BUILDING?
Once again, it depends. Boyshorts made of super-thin cotton, microfiber, or nylon don't add extra bulk. If you're not curvy on the bottom, and undie lines aren't a problem, go for it. But if you wear super-tight jeans and don't want a lot of fabric between you and your denim, choose a smaller pair of undies with less coverage.

4 WHICH BRA SHOULD I WEAR WITH A T-SHIRT?
Wear a nude bra with a smooth cup and an underwire under a white T-shirt, not a white one (you'll be able to see it!). Anything with seams, or decorative elements like embroidery, flowers, or bows will be visible underneath.

5 IF I'M SMALL ON TOP, DO I HAVE TO WEAR A BRA, OR IS A CAMISOLE OKAY?
That depends on how you feel about coverage. Bras keep your curves and your nipples covered, even when it's cold. The same can't be said for camisoles and tanks. But if you're okay with the natural look, or if you're wearing a bulky top or sweater, wear whatever makes you feel comfortable.

6 HOW LONG SHOULD UNDERPANTS LAST AND WHEN SHOULD I TOSS THEM OUT?
Whenever the elastic starts to give a little (it doesn't snap back into shape after washing, or it starts to fray), toss them! It's good to keep a couple of not-so-nice undies around for period days. But generally speaking, underwear is only built to last for a few months up to a year of wear and tear.

7 WHAT IF A NECKLINE OR ARMHOLES ARE SO LOW, A BRA WOULD BE TOO VISIBLE?
Try wearing a tank top or a camisole over your bra, or instead of a bra. It's okay if a little of that shows.

EVERYTHING YOU NEED TO KNOW ABOUT. . .
JACKETS & COATS

There are a few key coat shapes that look good on everyone, and can work with just about any outfit, while keeping you toasty and warm.

THREE UNIVERSAL COATS, FOR DAY, NIGHT, AND EVERYTHING IN BETWEEN

1 CROPPED BOMBER
It hits at the waist, or just above the hips, and has a fitted waistband. In leather, nylon, or wool, it works with jeans and skirts, daytime and night.

2 PEACOAT
Short or tall, curvy or narrow, a peacoat that hits just at or below the hips is the universally stylish, all-purpose coat. Originally a military-issued coat for sailors (which is why some of them have anchors on the buttons), a peacoat is made of wool with a double row of buttons up the front. Find one that isn't too boxy or bulky so it doesn't conceal your shape.

3 THREE-QUARTER-LENGTH COAT
Made of nylon, wool, or stuffed with down, a slightly A-line coat that hits mid-thigh to the knee and either zips or buttons up the front is a great choice for any body type. Buy one in a neutral color, like black, gray, tan, or dark red, so it goes with anything you own (a tone-on-tone pattern is also a good choice). Dress it up with a fur scarf for night, or go casual with a knit cap for day.

A leather bomber like Haylie Duff's is a timelessly cool look.

TIP: If you're short or curvy all over, you might not want a coat with a fitted waistband that cuts you off in the middle, exaggerating your shape or your smaller stature. Instead, look for a more tapered style that's longer and hits below the hip to mid-thigh.

Kelly Osbourne's coat doesn't match anything, so it sort of goes with everything.

The belt on this coat worn by Naomi Watts takes the bulk factor down a notch.

FOUR "NICE-TO-HAVE" EXTRA COATS

A puffy vest like **Erika Christensen's** can go with a dress and boots if you've got the right attitude.

1 SPRINGTIME JACKET

A lightweight jacket that suits your style is an in-between-weather staple. Anything goes: an army jacket, a belted coat with lots of chic pockets, a blazer shape, or a barn jacket.

2 PUFFY VEST

Over a sweatshirt or long sleeves, a vest is a great alternative for fall and spring when a full-size puffer seems stifling hot. It's perfect for school, weekends, or snowy sports, and is an all-around good investment.

This shiny black trench with a wide belt is a simple, glamorous coat that **Lindsay Lohan** will have for a lifetime.

Sarah Jessica Parker's classic trench will never go out of style.

Drew Barrymore's black trench has a slimming look.

Cropped sleeves add a modern touch to **Charlize Theron's** chocolate brown trench.

4 EVENING COAT

A button-up coat in lightweight wool, with brass or silver buttons or a stylish sash, is a good splurge. Buy a timeless style that isn't too trendy, and you'll have it for years to come.

3 TRENCH COAT

Scour thrift and consignment shops for an old-school trench coat. The shape has barely changed in decades! While brand-new ones are pricey, a second-hand version can be found on the cheap and is a really cool alternative to a regular rain slicker.

6 DETAILS,

DETAILS

Accessories

DETAILS, DETAILS

The little things in life, and in your closet, can make all the difference! Looking for a fast, easy, ridiculously fun and inexpensive way to quadruple your wardrobe choices? Focus on your accessories. Small details like sunglasses, necklaces, earrings, bracelets, scarves, hats, shoes, belts, and pins help define your style like nothing else and can work as quick-change tricks, switching up the style of an outfit in a snap. Even if you live life in jeans and T-shirts, the way you accessorize will help you stand out in a crowd.

Follow these accessories guidelines, and you'll never go wrong:

1. KNOW WHEN ENOUGH IS ENOUGH Dangling earrings, enormous sunglasses, piles of necklaces, stacks of bracelets, AND a 10-pound handbag? That is overkill. The rule is to take off one accessory before you leave the house.

2. DON'T BE A TREND VICTIM Even though accessories are the best way to stay up on trends without spending a ton of money, it's possible to overdo it. If you've got 7 charms dangling from your phone and 8 from the zipper of your bag, maybe you should take off a few (or, even better, rotate them!). There's a fine line between getting a trend right and wearing it to death. Try not to cross it. Consider Lindsay Lohan, who pushes trends as far as they can go before they start to look ridiculous.

Lindsay Lohan

3. FIND A SIGNATURE ACCESSORY One way to develop a recognizable style that's all your own is to find a special accessory and stick with it. For example, cowboy boots look great with jeans, minis, even shorts if you wear them the right way. Wear them a lot and all of a sudden, they become totally you! Whether it's a long, striped scarf, a cool hat, or a big strand of turquoise beads—find an accessory you love and wear it whenever you can.

4. DON'T BE AFRAID TO EXPERIMENT Think of the quirkiest dressers—like Sienna Miller, Chloe Sevigny, and Maggie Gyllenhaal—and what makes their style special. It's the way they put things together in a jumbly mix. That didn't happen overnight or by accident. We promise you that every outfit they "throw together" has required some serious time spent in front of the mirror. The key is not to be afraid to be different, because what's unique about you is what makes you special.

Andrea Bowen's **beads can make the transition from red-carpet to casual event.**

Q'Orianka Kilcher adds a blast of funky glamour to her outfit with these ocean-blue beads.

JEWELRY
TO SUIT ANY STYLE

It's the most personal accessory that you'll buy, and usually the most expensive, so choose carefully and invest wisely. A simple necklace made of precious metal, or a pair of pearl stud earrings, will never go out of style. Those three-inch-wide orange beads are a different story.

FREE SPIRIT

- Necklaces with beads or charms (worn two or three at a time) suit your style.
- Stacks of bangle bracelets may be impractical for some people, but a free spirit never lets something like that stand in her way.
- Ethnic-inspired earrings with crystals and chains or retro ones in plastic match your big-style personality.
- Look for a brightly-colored leather watchband with a classic face.

Lindsay Lohan

Keira Knightley

FEMININE AND FLIRTY

- Dangling earrings are both eye-catching and alluring.
- Gold or silver necklaces with charms or lockets show off your neckline.
- Look for bracelets with pearls, charms, or ribbons.
- Cocktail rings with big, colorful rhinestones are fun and flirty.
- Antique watches with tiny faces are a perfect match for your style.

HIGH GLAM

- Glamorous girls are drawn toward anything sparkly, like elaborate necklaces and dazzling bangles.
- Oversize earrings and bracelets with ethnic details add a seriously glam touch to any outfit.
- Necklaces and chains with oversize links add even more sizzle to your style.

Beyoncé

- Your ideal watch is jewelry-inspired, with a mother-of-pearl face or bracelet band.

MALIBU COOL

- Long gold necklaces with small charms look great over a ribbed tank top or a silky shirt at night.
- The easy style of thin metal bracelets appeals to you.

Jennifer Aniston

- Small earrings, like tiny hoops or studs, match your daytime-casual style. Anything that dangles but is still delicate will look right at night.
- A classic, sporty metal watch is a good choice.

TRUE ORIGINAL

- Anything goes—silk flowers, a granny necklace—if it's worn with confidence.
- Plastic earrings or big rhinestone hoops? The trick is to wear them with something unexpected, like sparkly stones with T-shirts or casual jewelry with dress-up clothes.

Gwen Stefani

- Carry a pocket watch—or go watch-free. You're not keeping to anyone else's schedule anyway.

DOWNTOWN ECCENTRIC

- Good-quality jewelry in unusual shapes is what the eccentric dresser craves. Get one great piece and wear it all the time.
- "Organic" shapes, inspired by things found in nature, appeal to your sophisticated style.
- Aside from the occasional strand of chunky beads, avoid anything large or obvious.

Nicole Richie

- A small, classic watch on a thin leather band that wraps around your wrist twice works with your eccentric look.

Samaire Armstrong

SEXY AND STRONG

- A nameplate necklace matches your edgy style.
- Bold earrings—oversize hoops or even a mismatched set—work best for you.
- A stack of thick rings suits you more than a sweet or delicate version.
- Try a man's steel watch with an oversize face, or one fastened to a leather cuff.

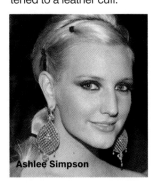

Ashlee Simpson

SWEET-NATURED REBEL

- Layers of heavyweight silver necklaces or chain-mail-inspired earrings add a rock-and-roll touch.
- Black leather is instantly rebellious, even tied with a bow or in a delicate shape. Studs look tough even with pink leather!
- Chunky rings suit your style. Nothing dainty will do.
- Your watch has a big face on a thick leather strap.

Paris Hilton

DESIGNER PRINCESS

- Any status symbol you can find, you love, whether it's a Chanel charm bracelet or an Hermès bangle.
- A tennis bracelet (real or fake) is a princess's best friend.
- Tasteful stud earrings with sparkly stones or big shimmering hoops are your everyday basics.
- Several necklaces of various lengths add a modern touch to a designer addict's outfit.
- As far as watches go, the more recognizable the brand, the better. Look for secondhand versions at a vintage jewelry shop.

**Warning: If you're label-obsessed, be prepared to pay the price. Even vintage and thrift shops are savvy enough to price these items accordingly. But because you are SO not alone in your obsession, discount and department stores generally see to it that they have copies of must-have designer label accessories. Consider the much cheaper knockoffs.

Sarah Jessica Parker

CLASSIC WITH A TWIST

- Charm bracelets were a big hit in the 1950s and have recently made quite a comeback. Buy one that's ready-made or collect charms to build your own.
- A strand of pearls, or two, will never go out of style.
- Delicate gold chains with simple charms and understated stones suit your subtle style.
- Small hoops decorated with diamonds or diamond studs have a classic look with a feminine edge.

SUNGLASSES
TO SUIT ANY STYLE

Lately, it seems like the bigger the sunglasses, the better. Oversize plastic frames have taken over as the shades of choice, no matter what your style may be.

FREE SPIRIT
Plastic glasses in wrap-around shapes with large lenses and black, green, or blue frames suit your free-spirited style.

Michelle Trachtenberg

FEMININE AND FLIRTY
Large plastic frames in slightly rounded shapes in tortoise (or even white or red) are the classic ladylike choice. If you want to be a little different, try a slightly retro cat-eyed shape.

Lindsay Lohan

Ashley Olsen

HIGH GLAM
Glasses with designer logos on the legs are a glam girl's signature. The bolder the logo, the better the glasses, in your view.

Natasha Bedingfield

MALIBU COOL
Large wraparound lenses tinted a light blue or soft rose are a big look in L.A., home of that beachy-cool style. Beachy girls also love '70s-inspired aviator shapes.

TRUE ORIGINAL
Colored lenses with rhine-stones in the corner, funny plastic shades from the flea market—nothing's too out-rageous for you.

Mariah Carey

DOWNTOWN ECCENTRIC
Either an aviator style with a silver frame or classic black Ray-Bans is a good match for a cool girl with an urban edge.

Nicky Hilton

Fergie

SEXY AND STRONG
Wraparound glasses and anything with major hard-ware, like gleaming metal frames and reflective lenses, have that edgy look you love. Try windshield-style frames that cover your eyes completely.

Eve

SWEET-NATURED REBEL
Oversize, bug-eyed rock star glasses in the blackest black are perfect for rebels. A super-cool alternative are darkly tinted aviators.

Nicole Richie

DESIGNER PRINCESS
Back in the '70s, huge round shades were everywhere. Snag a few cheap pairs in fun colors and change them according to your outfit.

Chloe Sevigny

CLASSIC WITH A TWIST
Tortoiseshell frames appeal to your traditional tastes. But beyond that, which shape you choose depends on the shape of your face. For sunglass inspiration, look to Jackie O.—she had more classic taste than anybody.

THE RIGHT SHAPE FOR YOUR FACE...

Before you choose the shades for you, find out which frames flatter your face. The general rule is to pick a shape that's the opposite of how your face is shaped. It's usually easier to determine your face shape if you look at a picture of your face, not to look at it in the mirror. In the mirror, lighting can affect the way you see your features and your face. A picture is more straightforward.

- If you have a SQUARE face with a strong jaw, find a pair of glasses that are slightly rounded, like oversize Jackie O. specs.

- If you have a ROUND or full face, rectangular glasses, like big Bono-style rock-star shades with squared-off edges, are best.

- If you have a HEART-SHAPED face (a narrow chin and a broad forehead), cat-eyed glasses that flare out a little at the top are an excellent choice, or even aviators that are broader at the top.

- If you have an OVAL face (equally wide at the forehead and near the chin), good news! You can wear any shape you want, but rectangular glasses with slightly rounded edges look best.

BELTS AND SCARVES
TO SUIT ANY STYLE

If you just want the basic belt and scarf wardrobe, you'll need two of each: an option for day and night. Then you can build from there.

FREE SPIRIT

- A thin belt that wraps around your waist twice, or an extra-thick one that sits on your hips, are two belt basics for a free-spirited fashion addict.

Keira Knightley

- Vintage scarves with bold patterns go around your head or can be wrapped around your wrist as a bracelet.

FEMININE AND FLIRTY:

- A large, square floral scarf can be tied around your head at the beach or on a shopping trip, around your neck for a dressier look, or around your waist to pinch-hit as a belt.

- Thick belts that cinch full skirts, or thin ones in velvet, accentuate your waist, which is a very feminine touch.

Rachel Bilson

Jennifer Lopez

HIGH GLAM

- Bold belts in metallic leather with big buckles, or fabric ones covered in sequins, aren't just for nights out if you're truly glam.

- Snuggle up in a fake fur scarf in winter, or tie on a Pucci-inspired silk number at the beach.

MALIBU COOL

- Your idea of dressing up is throwing a sequined scarf, in any color, over a white ribbed tank or a T-shirt, and it works.

Jessica Biel

- Look for thick leather belts with western-style buckles to wear with worn-in jeans.

TRUE ORIGINAL

- A graffiti print or a long scarf made of T-shirt fabric are made for original thinkers and dressers.

Cameron Diaz

- Eighties-inspired cloth belts with interlocking buckles or flea market finds in a rainbow of colors suit your unique taste.

DOWNTOWN ECCENTRIC

- A leather belt always comes in handy. Look for a second one in a wider cut to throw on over dresses or slouchy tops.
- Long and skinny is the scarf shape you love. A graphic print, a stripe, or a bold solid color will work with your wardrobe.

Eliza Dushku

SEXY AND STRONG

- Around your head and under a baseball cap is one way, since scarves aren't necessarily tough.
- A thick belt with a silver buckle makes a tough-enough statement for your street-inspired style.

Evangeline Lilly

SWEET-NATURED REBEL

- Leather belts with studs (either thick or thin widths, small or large studs) are mandatory for any fashion rebel.

- Try a skinny scarf with a metallic thread for a rock-and-roll touch, either day or night.

Hilary Duff

DESIGNER PRINCESS

- A belt with a flashy buckle, by Gucci or D&G or any number of other luxury brands, is your ideal belt. So is a chain belt in silver or gold.

Eva Longoria

- Status-y scarves from top-named designers in rich silk with bold patterns glam up a ponytail. Larger scarves fold into very glamorous halters for a night on the town.

CLASSIC WITH A TWIST

- Cinch your waist with a wide leather belt in a classic color.

- Fold a scarf into a 3-inch wide strip and use it as a headband. Tie it at the back of your neck and let the ends fall loosely down your back.

Shannon Elizabeth

TIP: Don't feel limited to just black or brown with belts. A bright red leather belt is actually a neutral color, worn with many different shoes (as long as you're not afraid to mix it up!).

105

HATS
TO SUIT ANY STYLE

Whether you wear a hat for fashion or function, pick one that's a perfect match for your personality.

Fergie

FREE SPIRIT
On questionable hair days, style-conscious girls prefer designer silk scarves to scruffy hats. In the winter, anything with earflaps or an intricately knit design won't go unnoticed.

Beyoncé

HIGH GLAM
A wide-brim floppy hat with a jeweled band suits your style. At night, a sparkly scarf, or anything shimmery, does the trick. For winter, furry earmuffs are the only option for a glam girl who doesn't want to flatten her 'do!

Gwen Stefani

TRUE ORIGINAL
Once again, anything goes, whether it's a knit Rasta hat or an old fedora. When it's cold, the bigger the better: furry hats make a big statement in winter.

Eva Mendes

SEXY AND STRONG
You love baseball caps, and at night, the same styles (with a little added sparkle) do the trick. In the winter, try a newsboy cap in tweed for a warmer take on the tomboy look.

Michelle Trachtenberg

DOWNTOWN ECCENTRIC
A man's fedora adds an unexpected twist to a black tie look, or a jeans and T-shirt outing. In the winter, a chunky knit hat in an unexpected color or stripes has an Indie-rock feel.

Rachel Bilson

FEMININE AND FLIRTY
A floppy hat is a good match for the floral dresses and sweet tops you love. In the winter, a cozy hat with a pom-pom speaks to your girly side.

Scarlett Johanssen

MALIBU COOL
You really only wear hats to shield yourself from the sun, and a cotton fishing hat (on the smaller side) is a good option. For cooler weather, a knit cap does the trick.

Ziyi Zhang

DESIGNER PRINCESS
A jeweled beret or newsboy cap is a suitably glamorous choice. During the winter, a fur hat (fake, of course!) is the right touch.

Sienna Miller

SWEET-NATURED REBEL
A train engineer's cap is the ideal topper to your denim-heavy wardrobe. When it gets cold, a dark knit cap does the trick.

Amanda Bynes

CLASSIC WITH A TWIST
A bucket hat is a good, slightly preppy look for summer days. When it's cold, a classic beret is understated and so cute.

DRESS-UP SHOES
TO SUIT ANY STYLE

Ahhhh, shoes. Who doesn't love them? While it's tempting to snatch up every great pair you see, if you have just one or two great dress-up options, you can throw them on with nearly anything. Treat bold colors like bright pink, electric blue, or even animal prints as basics—no matter what your style—and we promise: your look will never be dull.

Eva Longoria

Reese Witherspoon

Ashanti

FREE SPIRIT

Cowboy boots are a free-spirited staple; so are wooden-soled sandals with fabric straps. Any shoe with a personality as big as yours is the perfect pick.

FEMININE AND FLIRTY

Medium- to high-heeled sandals in bright colors or patterns (either leather or fabric), or pointy-toe flats in equally interesting shades, suit your fun and feminine sense of style.

HIGH GLAM

Jeweled sandals with towering heels are a year-round staple for glamazons, who wear them with dresses, jeans, everything. If you want to cover up a little more, try wearing towering knee-high boots in shiny velvet or bright-colored suede with silky dresses or pulled up over jeans.

107

Q'Orianka Kilcher

Sienna Miller

Nicole Richie

Lindsay Lohan

MALIBU COOL
Boots with low-to-medium heels give even the dressi-est outfits a casual feel. When you need to dress it up a little more, try a pair of strappy gold sandals.

TRUE ORIGINAL
Try wedge-heeled pumps or sandals in outrageous prints or unusual patterns, like

brightly-colored florals, zebra stripes, or leopard spots.

DOWNTOWN ECCENTRIC
A pair of simple black flats worn with jeans, dresses, even leggings, is as cool as it gets.

SEXY AND STRONG
Slouchy boots that are pushed down to gather at

the ankle are a tough-chic girl's best friend. Try metallic or velvet sneakers if heels aren't your thing. Wearing the occasional pair of heels, with toes that are round instead of pointy, won't sac-rifice comfort for style.

SWEET-NATURED REBEL
Boots—either ankle-high or up to the knee, with heels,

are a nighttime staple for just about any time of year. So are black or silver wedge heels. In the sum-mer, try gladiator-style san-dals that wrap around your ankle and calf.

DESIGNER PRINCESS
There isn't a heel too high or a toe too pointy for a true designer princess, who loves shoes with extra baubles, beads, or flowers sewn on—whatever's fash-ionable that minute.

CLASSIC WITH A TWIST
Satin pumps with round toes are as ladylike as they come. Match your shoes to your dress if you want a pulled-together, tailored look. Black and white spec-tator pumps are another classic choice. Kitten-heeled silvery sandals with delicate straps are an all-season staple, and go well with bold-patterned floral dresses that are often hard to match.

Christina Milian

Shakira

Taryn Manning

WHOSE SHOES?

Can you guess which shoes belong to your favorite celebrities?

1. Towering, be-decked sandals like these are fit for hip-hop and pop's reigning queen, which is why she's wearing them!

2. The stunning celeb who owns these pointy-toed stilettos doesn't need any help with her height from these extra-tall sandals.

3. These shiny silver pumps are a relatively low-key choice for this Texan songstress!

4. These high boots with a chic buckle look like they could kick some butt, but the buttery brown suede shows their softer side—just like their owner, who's tough on screen and sweet on the red carpet.

5. Round-toe satin pumps are a very subdued choice for their usually racy owner.

6. Even if these jeweled stilettos were made of pure gold, the singer who's wearing them could afford it!

7. No doubt these knee-high velvet boots on this star's feet cost more than most people's rent.

8. Black-and-white spectator pumps like these are usually reserved for more, well, reserved starlets. This wild child is showing her more reserved side at this event.

9. These black velvet pumps are a good choice for this fashion all-star who's been spending a lot of time at the beach lately.

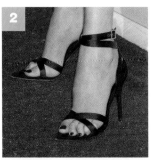

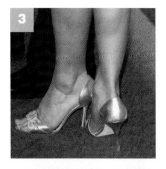

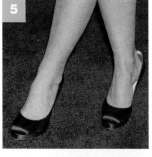

ANSWERS

1: Beyoncé. 2: Charlize Theron. 3: Jessica Simpson. 4: Jennifer Garner. 5: Carmen Electra. 6: Ashanti. 7: Rosario Dawson. 8: Lindsay Lohan. 9: Mischa Barton.

109

ALL-TIME ACCESSORIES
ALLSTARS!

There are a couple of lessons we can learn from these 4 celebrities, even though their looks are so different. One is that less is not always more. When most people might stop at just one or two accessories, these ladies go all out, wearing whatever strikes their fancy that day. The other? Fashion isn't something you should be afraid of. If you take a big risk, you get a big reward.

KEIRA KNIGHTLEY A self-professed tomboy, Keira Knightley has an accessories style that's hard to beat. Whether she's low-key in boots, jeans, and beads, or glamourous in a form-fitting gown accented with an arm cuff and exotic earrings, she's herself, and she's beautiful.

SARAH JESSICA PARKER

There doesn't seem to be any accessory Parker can't wear—or doesn't own. From rubber rain boots to diamonds to enormous designer bags, she's got the stocked closet everyone wishes they had. In a classic trench coat or a couture gown straight from the runway, she makes every look her own with her irreverent sense of style.

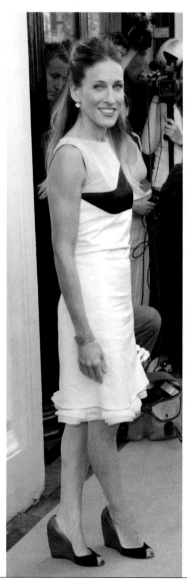

ALICIA KEYS

Whether she's experimenting with sunglasses, piles of jewelry, skirts over pants, long braids, or pinning a cascade of flowers to her hair for the red carpet, Alicia Keys knows how to make a statement all her own. She has proven, again and again, that understated accessories aren't the only way to go.

RACHEL BILSON

With her rockin' jewelry and irreverent style, this seriously cute star has taught us to take some chances with our look. No matter where she goes, she looks casually cool, thanks to her unusual jewelry, taste for vintage bags, and weakness for great shoes.

7

SPECIAL

EVENT
Style

SPECIAL EVENT STYLE

Working your personal style at homecoming, prom, holidays, family functions, special dates, big birthdays, or your cousin Mike's wedding isn't as hard as it seems. Pair a drop-dead dress with a funky scarf. Match oversized vintage earrings with a simple gown. Pile on three necklaces to spice up a strapless dress. Remember: Big nights out can be about trying out "iconic" looks—classically elegant, glam rocker, red-carpet starlet—without overhauling your whole wardrobe.

Here are some tips for hassle-free special event style:

1. Make sure your outfit is right for the occasion! While it might be fun to rock out with a dress decorated with punky safety pins at the school dance, it's not the best choice for a family wedding—especially if you upstage the bride in pictures!

2. It's tempting to spend a fortune on your outfit, but resist the urge. We know how important special events can be, but the splurge factor has gotten a little out of control. Be smart with your spending and buy things that you might be able to wear again, like gold or silver shoes instead of pumps dyed to match your bright-blue dress that will sit in the closet for the rest of eternity. Or a beaded handbag that can be used year after year, not just one night only.

3. Get creative with the dresses you own. If you have a long gown that you don't wear anymore, think about having it hemmed to a cocktail or knee length. Look for beaded tops that you can throw over a dress you already own to change the look altogether. Chances are, no one will notice that you've worn that dress before. And if your close friends do, they'll be impressed with how you've changed the look with your inventive style.

Trading in her casual jeans for a ruffled white gown, Kate Beckinsale embraces her inner green siren.

Jessica Alba lets her elegant side shine through in this flowing charcoal gray dress.

CLASSIC
BLACK DRESSES

There have been entire books written about black dresses because they've been a standby for fancy parties for decades. What they say is true. Every stylish lady needs at least one of these in her wardrobe.

EMMA ROBERTS
Let us count the ways we love this dress: 1. It's effortlessly stylish, thanks to the luxe fabric and perfect fit. 2. It's simple and cool, not overdone. 3. It works for so many body types, creating curves on straight-up-and-down frames (thanks to the fitted bodice), baring shoulders but not too much cleavage for anyone with curves on top (because of the straight-across bustline), and flattering curvy-on-the-bottom figures with a loosely cut gathered skirt. Plus, the below-the-knee length works if you're petite or tall. In short, it's perfection!

LEANN RIMES
Timeless is the best way to describe this dress. The delicate pleats, the narrow straps and low sweetheart neckline, the flattering fitted waist and loose bodice, and the slight A-line skirt add up to a dress that will never go out of style. If you're small on top and curvy on the bottom, or are looking to create curves, look for a style similar to this one. At an inch or two below the knee, it's the most universally flattering length (and it works for formal or semiformal events). Also, if you want to show off strong arms and shoulders, or create curves on a narrow bod, this is an excellent shape to do it.

LINDSAY LOHAN
With its high neckline, cap sleeves, body-skimming satiny fabric, and gathers around the hips that really accentuate curves, this 1930s-inspired cocktail dress has an old-Hollywood appeal. Because of the way the fabric drapes, a dress like this one looks best on someone who has the curves—both on top and on the bottom—to fill it out, and isn't afraid to show them. The slightly below-the-knee length looks better with heels than flats.

RACHEL BILSON
Rachel gets her proportions just right yet again: The above-the-knee length makes her legs look longer, and the high neckline and sleeves add just the right balance to make this a sweet (but still sexy) choice for petite frames. It's the curve-skimming fabric that keeps this dress looking cute, not too baggy or conservative. And it's a great blank canvas to dress up with accessories. Pair it with unusual shoes, like she does, or add a few strands of colorful beads or bold earrings.

- Look for a simple shift or a strapless dress that falls to the knee. This is the most timeless dress you'll ever buy! If you're going for a classic look, wear it with an up do, a vintage-y rhinestone necklace and black shoes. If that's too classic for your look, throw on a sequined scarf. It's kind of like a blank canvas, and you can dress it up any way you want with accessories.

- If you don't want to show off your arms, look for a dress with short sleeves that's fitted everywhere else. If you are curvy on the bottom, find one with a fuller skirt and an open top to draw attention to your pretty shoulders.

- Find one in a fabric that works in any season, like silk, satin, or a lightweight wool crepe instead of wool or velvet that's too heavy for warmer weather.

VANESSA CARLTON

The inventive sleeves and body-skimming cut of this sophisticated dress make it a fantastic pick for curvy bodies. The elbow-length sleeves are flattering on a broad upper body, and the straight-across bustline still shows some skin, but gives enough coverage for a large bust (without looking frumpy). The length and the elegant fabric, rich and subtle looking, make this another classic choice that will never go out of style.

REESE WITHERSPOON

An asymmetrical hemline is the fastest way to flatter full hips. The diagonal line creates more length on your bottom half, making legs seem longer and leaner. The gathers on the side (called "shirring") will camouflage a little belly. Well-placed lace along the bustline hints at the curves beneath without showing too much skin, making it an ideal neckline for curvy tops. A dress with a busy hemline on bottom needs a simple top, like these straightforward straps. If you're curvy all over and aren't afraid to show some skin, look for a dress with similar details.

EMMY ROSSUM

This looks like a dancer's dress, with a full skirt and a top that hugs the body. This fabric clings to every bump and curve, so if you have a whole lot (or very little) on top, choose a material with less stretch. But if you're slimmer on top and want to show it off (or de-emphasize a curvier bottom half), a dress like this does the trick. Skip the skinny rhinestone belt if you want, and try a wide, waist-cinching belt in a bold color like red, violet, or royal blue instead. Wear flat slippers to work the ballerina look, or try strappy sandals that tie around the ankles.

NATALIE PORTMAN

Half sweet, half sexy, 100% gorgeous: Rich details like feminine black lace, a sweetheart bustline and a jeweled, waist-cinching belt make this strapless dress a head-turner. The lacy bodice shows off her shoulders and makes her shape look curvier. The belt detail calls attention to a slender waist (or creates the look of one on straighter bodies). Larger busts may spill out over the structured bodice, so if you're curvy on top, beware. Understated accessories are a must—any additional fuss could take this stunner from girlish to garish.

HEAD-TURNING COLOR

A black dress is always a classic, and a safe, tasteful choice, but there's nothing like a fuchsia, scarlet, or lime-green dress if you want to be noticed. The downside? You may get more attention than you'd like. Wear look-at-me colors with confidence, and it'll be a night you'll never forget.

SCARLETT JOHANSSEN

This curve-clinging bright red gown is a "show 'em what you've got" style, but is sophisticated at the same time. Since this dress is so simple, it takes curves to bring it to life; on narrow frames, it may fall flat.

ZIYI ZHANG

With the lemon-lime color and light-as-air tulle skirt, it looks like she could float—in a good way. The fitted bodice and sweetheart neckline make her waist look tiny and her curves feminine. This shape works for nearly everyone, but those with a curvy top or broad upper body may find it doesn't offer the coverage or support they need.

JESSICA ALBA

Who says you need to show skin at a special event? The short sleeves, knee-length skirt, and ruffle details make this a sweet choice for a big night. What keeps it from looking too young is the open neckline and intense turquoise color. This dress has just the right proportions for someone curvy on top with broad shoulders and narrower hips (the full skirt balances the bottom with the top). This shape will flatter just about anyone, though the waist-cinching belt could call attention to a thicker middle.

ALICIA SILVERSTONE

This fuchsia satin dress has a simple shape, and it could pass as an everyday dress without the sheen. The cap sleeves, high neckline, just-below-the-knee length and A-line skirt make this dress a comfortable, body-friendly choice for lots of shapes. If you're curvy all over, the plain, detail-free satin may reveal too much of what's underneath.

- Vivid bright colors like violet, magenta, and leaf green look best in warmer, summer months. Deep jewel tones, like ruby red, plum, or emerald green are better for winter parties.

- Don't feel like you need to get shoes and a bag to match your dress exactly. Bright colors look great with silver or gold accents. Deeper jewel tones also work with black. Evening bags with colorful beads or a pattern are also a good alternative, especially if the color of your dress is picked up in the print.

- If you're feeling really bold, try wearing sandals that contrast with the color of your dress, like bright coral with pale pink, intense green with blue, or navy with violet for an unexpected twist.

JOJO
Cute, cool, and a little bit clinging, this is a fun dress that's got serious style. The ruched fabric (see the way it's bunched up?) creates curves—perfect for anyone who's got a narrow, straight form. (On the other hand, not great for curves, which may make the fabric bunch or pull too much.)

QUEEN LATIFAH
The double straps and generous cut on top show off curves, but still provide enough coverage. The body-skimming fabric and skirt with a little fullness at the bottom are straight enough to show off your figure without adding bulk, and loose enough to be comfortable and not reveal too much. This dress works beautifully for almost any frame.

EVA LONGORIA
A column of color from the shoulders to the floor has a lengthening effect, and the gathered fabric around the hips flatters curves. Be careful if you don't want to show off your shoulders, since the asymmetrical halter top draws attention to bare skin around the arms and neck.

EVANGELINE LILLY
The thick straps and deep V-shaped neckline on this turquoise gown make it a perfect choice for anyone with strong, broad shoulders like hers. The fitted waist and the gather of fabric at the front, spilling out into a big, full skirt, make this a super-flattering shape if you're curvy all over.

HEY, LADY!

VINTAGE-INSPIRED DRESSES ARE TIMELESS AND PRETTY.

With cinched waists, fitted bodices, and full skirts, it's no wonder those '50s-inpsired dresses are here to stay. They make so many body types look good: Curvy bottoms get extra coverage, narrow bodies get instant curves, curvy-all-over types get an extra hourglass boost. For a big night on the town when you want to feel like a princess, there's no better choice.

EMMY ROSSUM

Emmy is fulfilling her sugar plum fairy fantasy with this dress, which could pass as a costume from *The Nutcracker*. It's light as air, and the full tulle skirt would make anyone feel like a lady. The tiny straps and shallow neckline make this dress a little too delicate for anyone who needs extra support on top, and the skirt may be just a tad too full and long for a petite person, but it's just right for her body—narrow on top and curvy on the bottom.

PARIS HILTON

In this sweet dress, Paris Hilton looks as cute and innocent as a baby chick! The sweetheart neckline and fitted bodice create ladylike curves on her narrow upper body, and the fullness of the skirt creates a nice hourglass shape. A full skirt that dips in the back can conceal extra curves, but the ruffle details on it could add more bulk to the lower body.

SCARLETT JOHANSSEN

No matter how demure a dress is, Scarlett finds a way to flaunt what she's got. With a different bra, this would be a very sweet 1950s-inspired look that offers ample coverage for curves, but the extra boost adds stare-at-me sex appeal that you've got to have the confidence to handle. The generous straps, fitted waist, and medium-full skirt make this dress ideal for women with full curves (or anyone who wants to pretend she does for a night).

REESE WITHERSPOON

Reese is back to her old tricks with this supremely ladylike dress. The demure tank-style top, fitted bodice, tight waist, and full skirt are flattering and discreet and don't scream for attention. It's a classic, timeless look that would compliment any shape. Because of the high neckline and the contrast between the white and the sequins, it could make a small bust look even smaller, so if you're looking to enhance your curves, another neckline might work better.

- Look for the right neckline for your body type. A sweetheart neckline that dips low at your breastbone and is rounded over your curves, is good if you're smaller on top. If you're trying to contain your curves, try a neckline that is straight across on top, or covers up your chest entirely with a sleeveless bodice.

- To keep from looking too sugary sweet, or like an extra from *Grease,* keep jewelry, makeup and accessories to a minimum: a pair of stud earrings, a bracelet and your everyday hairstyle, or a simple up-do with feminine dangling earrings. White gloves, bright lipstick, and vintage jewelry plus a '50s dress are way too retro when they're all worn together.

- For a school dance, request an old-fashioned wrist corsage to go with your dress, like a big fluffy mum or a peony, or a cluster of rosebuds.

JESSICA ALBA

This dress is 95% lady and 5% tramp (in a good way). Jessica has quite a body, and she isn't going to hide it. The black lace overlay is a nice ladylike touch, as is the ribbon-tied belt that emphasizes her narrow waist. It's a lovely shape and length that flatters any figure, with equal parts sass and class.

KATHARINE HEIGL

This isn't only "inspired by" the '50s and early '60s, it really looks like it's from that era. The at-the-knee length, high waist, high cowl neckline, and pea-green overlay are all telltale signs of a vintage dress. This shape can look frumpy on even the slenderest frames, and the high waist and tight front aren't the best for exaggerated curves. But this can be a good length and shape if you're tall, and Katharine pulls it off.

CARRIE UNDERWOOD

A little bit sweet, a little bit sparkly, a lot glamorous, this dress is a real winner. (The shell-pink ribbon belt is also a personal touch that can be added to any dress with a fitted waist.) The sequins clustered at the top put the focus on the upper body. The A-line skirt that hits mid-calf is an old-fashioned length that's elegant and timeless. Short or tall, thick or thin, this is a nice option that brings out anybody's inner princess.

WILLA HOLLAND

Even though she's still a young teenager, Willa's got an impressive, sophisticated style. And this dress matches both her girlish side and her fashion sense. The narrow belt enhances her waist, the gathered fabric over her shoulders and knee-length skirt bare just enough skin, and the black and white pattern has a breezy, ladylike feel to it. This is a dress that would flatter any body.

FUN AND FUNKY

PUT AN ORIGINAL SPIN ON FORMAL CLOTHES.

A corset top with knickers to the prom? A top hat with your party dress? Why the heck not? There's no reason to be so serious about formal wear. Throw on a pair of high top sneakers with your dress if you feel like taking a risk. There's no point in sacrificing your original style for a dressy party, as long as it's occasion-appropriate.

EVA MENDES

This oversize leaf pattern has got Palm Beach written all over it. It feels vintage, but it's not. And it definitely makes a statement. The floor-length, strapless, loosely-fitted style looks great on taller frames, but can make petite figures feel overwhelmed, and anyone with curvy, voluptuous bodies feel like they're hiding under all of that fabric.

MARY-KATE OLSEN

Red sandals, dangly earrings, and stacks of gold bangles give this vintage-feeling dress the right touch of glamour. Mary-Kate is known for making unpredictable fashion choices, and this is right in step with her style. The fitted bodice with a straight-across bustline is good for anyone who's small and narrow on top (like Mary-Kate) and may be too revealing for someone who isn't. The fuller skirt is more forgiving for curves on the bottom. Since you can see her feet, it means it's a good length if you're petite: Columns that go straight to the ground can take away from your height.

ANNE HATHAWAY

The empire waist (which means it hits at the rib cage) and longer sleeves make this style a good choice for anyone who feels better covered up, but still wants a fun, young dress that doesn't look frumpy. The half-sleeves make arms look lean. And the criss-cross top is flattering for everybody. As a finishing touch, boots are always a cool, unexpected choice for a special event.

- Try to put a different spin on your outfit with unusual accessories, like a hat, a necklace made of big colorful beads, bright fishnet stockings, or a pair of pink suede cowboy boots. Pick one wild thing and go for it, but steer clear of looking costumey by keeping the rest of your outfit (relatively) tame.

- Look for the things you like to wear in a more formal fabric. Do you love to wear hoodies? Why not find one in cashmere, and put it over a beaded skirt and strappy sandals for your next big event. Try satin shorts with dressy tights and heels, paired with a blousy top.

- Check out your local vintage stores for other unexpected ideas, like a floor-length crocheted dress from the '70s, a satin jump suit, or a dress with a graphic print that will definitely stand out in a crowd.

ASHLEY OLSEN

Is she wearing a jumpsuit, with shorts? Why yes, she is. And Ashley can really pull it off. The black satiny fabric makes the whole outfit look dressier than you'd expect. The short-shorts make her legs look longer. Anyone with major curves might be busting out of the seams of this getup, but if you're narrow or petite, and you like to break fashion rules, this is a good way to do it.

SOPHIE OKONEDO

This is a statement-making dress if we've ever seen one, in dramatically contrasting black and yellow. Because the neckline dips low, and the shoulders are bare, it really shows off her upper body. There's enough fabric to offer coverage on top for larger busts, and the contrast of solid black against the gold print can create the look of curves. The stripes on the bottom draw your eye to the floor, so if you're short, look for a style with a simpler skirt.

MAGGIE GYLLENHAAL

Maggie's an original who loves unique clothes. Is this a top over a dress, or part of the dress? Who knows? Who cares? The Japanese-inspired details and sunset colors are a break from basic black. The neckline is flattering, the sash carves out a slender waistline, and the cap sleeves make arms look longer and slimmer. This is a great look for all shapes—and especially anyone who isn't afraid to stand out in a crowd.

FLIRTY SKIRTS
Tops and bottoms can be mixed

There are so many good reasons to wear a skirt and a top to a special event. It's easier to dress for your body type—you can buy the right size of each and avoid a lot of hassle. It's more versatile and practical than a fancy dress. Why spend all of your money on a dress you may wear only once, when you could buy a top and a skirt that you can wear separately over and over—and can be so comfortable you'll want to stay at the party all night? Convinced?

SELMA BLAIR
She's covering so much skin, but look how long and lean Selma looks in this black color palette! It's a great winter look that creates curves on her narrow frame. The full skirt, wide belt, and turtleneck combine to give her a real hourglass shape. Someone with more significant curves might feel that the cinched belt and high neck over-emphasizes her bust, and the tight fitted skirt could reveal a bulging belly.

ALEXIS BLEDEL
Alexis is working a 1940s look with this outfit with the flowy sleeves and ruffled hem of the top, the curvy skirt with low pleats, and the pearls. The skirt has the added benefit of wide pinstripes, which can make hips look narrower and legs look longer. But anything that's fitted in the hips runs the risk of making lower bodies look wider. Since Alexis is tall and slender, this medium-width belt works, but a softer, ribbon version would look more fashion-forward and may not chop her off so abruptly in the middle.

KELLY OSBOURNE
The trumpet shape of this skirt makes Kelly look womanly and curvy, and she is famous for being comfortable with her regular-girl shape. The hip-length top she's paired with it makes her look longer and leaner than a shorter one would. And the cap sleeves and slightly flared hem of the skirt really emphasize her curvy shape, and could work the same magic on straight-up-and-down bodies.

and matched.

- For a cozy alternative to strapless dresses, try a beaded camisole, tank top, or short sleeve sweater with a beaded skirt. And that top will be worn again and again, with less-formal skirts, with dress pants, or jeans.

- If you're not sure you want to take the plunge and buy a dress with a full skirt, the skirt alone is a good place to start. Buy a big ball skirt that reaches all the way to the floor if you want to. If you wear it with a more casual top, it won't be over the top.

- Skirts that stop at the knee—the skirt-length "sweet spot"—are flattering for all shapes and sizes.

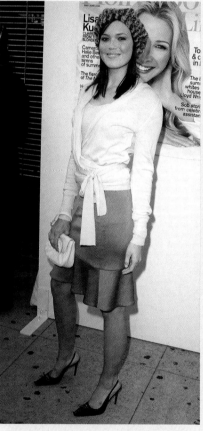

DEVON AOKI

For petite Devon, who's tiny all over, it makes sense to wear a skirt with rich detail and a solid top. The lace print brings out the curves of her lower half and the tight tank flatters her narrow top, adding a little oomph to her upper body. This look could also work with larger curves on top, but not on the bottom, because patterns can make the body part they cover appear bigger. For another night out, she could pair that skirt with a black turtleneck sweater or a white tank for a whole new look.

MANDY MOORE

This is a really sophisticated look for Mandy. The trumpet skirt with pleats along the hem that hits right at the knee emphasizes her pretty curves. And the wrap sweater with a deep, open V calls attention to a narrow waist. This look can work for anyone, though someone with a curvier lower half may choose to go with a darker color, since this light tan can make an area appear larger. A cropped tweed jacket and lacy camisole would be another great way to spice up this skirt.

LINDSAY LOHAN

Lindsay has had both straight-up-and-down and curvy-on-top body types. Here she's in a narrower phase, so this pencil skirt that falls straight to the knee is a good choice, and is really a grown-up sophisticated shape for anyone. On a curvier body, a pencil skirt fills out to a much sexier shape, so if that's the look you're after, it's a good pick. The sequined top is an easy way to dress up any skirt. This one is pretty revealing; experiment with different necklines to find the one that works for your shape.

PUNK PRINCESS *Make your rock star debut.*

Of all of the awards shows out there, we like the music events the best. Every year, someone wears the most outrageous outfit you could imagine, and no one even blinks. While we're not suggesting you arrive in a sequined bikini top, or a satin tracksuit, you can take a risk or two with leather jewelry, spiky boots, or safety pin earrings.

ASHLEE SIMPSON
Platinum-blond hair and jet-black clothes are two staples of rock-rebel style, and Ashlee wears both pretty well. This sparkly beaded minidress bares a lot of skin, so anyone with curves more prominent than hers may feel over-exposed. By wearing knee-high stockings with her heels, she adds even more edge to the look, which could look cute (but really young) on a petite frame. In general, tall people might steer clear of this look since it may be too cutesy to pull off.

MISCHA BARTON
This look is for someone who likes her legs, and mini-loving Mischa clearly does. The asymmetrical hem gives it a sexy-rebel feel, but the jacket, all unfinished edges and angular lines, makes the outfit. A fresh update on the classic motorcycle jacket, it's a stylish, slightly rebellious choice for a big night. The jacket offers enough coverage to make any body type feel comfortable—never dowdy—and the dress makes sure legs take center stage.

VANESSA CARLTON
There's nothing hard-core about Vanessa's music, but this dress she's wearing certainly has a punk side, thanks to the plaid print. Her long dark hair and strands of beads also give this look cool-girl cred. The seam details in the front and the A-line skirt have a slimming effect, and the straight-across bustline flatters fuller chests, so this style is a great choice for curvy-on-top and curvy-all-over body types.

- Even if your dress is colorful, jet black accessories make anything look edgier. Try knee-high black boots under your gown with a cuff bracelet.
- Hair and makeup can really change the look of an outfit. Braid the sides of your hair, pouf up the bangs and pull it into a ponytail for a rock and roll look, or add a bright blue hair extension for a punky touch. Some dramatic black, bright green or blue eyeliner and a slick of lipgloss are great finishing touches.
- The original punks in 1970s London wore plaid pants and jackets, clothes held together with safety pins and beat-up leather. Incorporate any of these ideas into your look, like a row of safety pins up the seam of your dress, a plaid taffeta mini-dress with a rockstar hairstyle and ankle boots, or a leather motorcycle jacket over your dress for instant rock cred.

MILLA JOVOVICH

This dress breaks every rule of traditional formal dressing. First, it's a print, which is usually reserved for daytime. Second, the top (which is sort of grandma-inspired) and skirt (which shows serious leg) don't look like they're parts of the same dress! But together, they're as cool as it gets. The proportions flatter short or tall figures, curves on top or broad shoulders. If you're curvy all over, but love to show off your legs, this is an excellent, unexpected choice.

ZOOEY DESCHANEL

The bubble skirt, mini-length, and black-and-blue color combination give this outfit its indie style. It's ladylike, but definitely has an edge, just like Zooey herself. The exaggerated, poufy style could give narrow bodies the appearance of curves, and it works if you're short or tall—especially with the dark stockings, which cover up some skin and keep the dress from looking too "sweet." But it's not the best choice for curves on the bottom, because the balloon skirt adds bulk.

KATE HUDSON

Kate's letting her true style show through with this edgy, unusual look. The black lace, long beads, low-slung belt, knee-high boots, and mini-skirt are all standard rock-and-roll details, which say "she's with the band" loud and clear. This red-carpet rebel look is suitable for nearly any body type, since the proportions are balanced (though for a real-life look, you might want to skip the long train in the back).

MALIBU COOL *It's laid-back but still luxe.*

Jennifer Aniston always looks like the coolest woman at the party, and it's her effortless approach that makes her look so good. She leaves her hair loose and wears dresses that look as comfortable as pajamas. The next time you have to dress up, don't feel pressure to spray your hair into some weird style or pile on jewelry. Try the laid-back approach instead: Choose a dress that's as comfy as an old T-shirt, and just add a little more polish to your everyday look.

ELISHA CUTHBERT

Throwing a jacket over any dress gives it an unexpected casual-cool edge. This slinky peach dress that hits mid-calf looks as comfortable as a nightgown, and would work for nearly any body type, as long as you don't mind calling attention to a shapely bottom half (the short jacket and shirring on the skirt can exaggerate your hips and bum). Elisha's look proves that just-washed hair and a little extra coverage can be sexy and sophisticated.

CHARLIZE THERON

It takes confidence and poise to pull off a dress that could look like a sleeping bag. And Charlize wears this cozy, strapless dress well. Short, petite frames would get lost in all of this fabric, and anyone with more exaggerated curves could feel like a sack of potatoes underneath it. But if you're tall and lean and you place comfy and cool at the top of your special-event priority list, then this is a style for you.

WILLA HOLLAND

Get the maximum out of a minidress, like knockout-in-the-making Willa Holland, by keeping it simple. The short sleeves, high neckline, and flat shoes keep a super-short dress looking sweet, not overly sexy. Tall girls with long legs like hers look even lankier in an abbreviated skirt, and the length and proportions of this dress are also a good choice if you're petite.

- Throw a favorite jacket or sweater over your evening gown, like a fitted canvas blazer or a cozy cardigan. This sends the message that cozy, familiar comfort is what's most important to you, even when it's time to play dress up. With a simple clutch and great shoes to keep everything dressy, you can't go wrong.

- When it comes to laidback dressing for a special event, loose and drapey beats tight and clingy every time. A dress that just skims over your body, or falls loose under the bust like an empire waist does, makes moving around and sitting a breeze. If you feel comfortable, you'll look comfortable.

- Keep your jewelry to a minimum, like a simple stack of narrow, gold-toned bangle bracelets, a thin gold chain, and some delicate dangling earrings. Or just wear a silver cuff bracelet and a pair of studs.

- If you wear your hair long and loose, try setting it with big hot rollers for smooth, pretty curls. If your hair is short, blow it dry into a sleeker style than you'd normally wear, like a smooth bob with a pretty rhinestone hair pin tucked behind one ear. Or just slick it back into a low ponytail. The trick is not to overdo it.

JENNIFER ANISTON
Jen practically invented Malibu-cool style: No matter what the occasion, chances are she'll wear her hair down and choose a body-skimming dress in an understated color. With its high neckline and knee-length skirt, this dress works for lots of bodies, as it covers up cleavage but still reveals the curves beneath. Anyone with a broad upper body may shy away from halter tops, and the heavy beaded fabric may cling too close for someone who's curvy all over.

JOY BRYANT
Joy's flowing, loose-fitting dress that skims the ground behind her is the perfect example of laid-back luxury. It's easy to wear, exposing enough skin to be young and sexy, and offers enough coverage to make it look like it's not trying too hard. The fabric falls loosely over the body, so it skims over wider hips, or makes slender figures look feminine and curvier.

CHRISTINA MILIAN
With simple accessories and undone hair, this dress strikes the right balance between understated and elegant. The deep V and medium-width fabric at the shoulders flatter broad shoulders, and keep from revealing too much (making it a good choice for curvy bodies). This dress looks so comfy that you can see her wearing it over a pair of jeans for a less formal night out.

WEAR THE PANTS *Put an unexpected twist on a*

Designer Yves Saint Laurent, famous for dressing up ladies in 1970s Paris in black tuxedos, made wearing pants to black-tie parties the chicest thing in town. If a whole tuxedo seems too grown up and serious for you, try wearing just the pants with a fancy top instead. It's comfortable, stylish, and a great alternative for anyone who wouldn't be caught dead in a skirt!

ALICIA KEYS
With something this revealing on top, it's a good idea to wear something simple on the bottom, which is what Alicia Keys did. A bold pattern like this draws your eye to the upper body, and black pants take a backseat, so it's a way to pair pants and tops if you're curvier on the bottom. This halter looks like it's barely hanging on, though, so someone with a larger bust may need to find something more substantial.

JULIA STILES
This is another perfect pick for nearly any body type, though Julia's legs would look longer if you could see more of her shoes under the hem of these pants. The V-shaped neckline creates length on her upper body and hints at her curves, just like the sheer fabric. But the lace camisole is a sweet and discreet touch. All in all, it's a look that works for narrow or curvy girls.

REESE WITHERSPOON
Black from head to toe—and pants!—are two unusual choices for Reese, who can usually be spotted in super-ladylike clothes. The puffy sleeves, slim pants, and belt with silver accents give this look a girlish feel. Once again, wearing the same color (especially black) on top and bottom makes you look long and lean. This is a good pick for any figure, but it may call extra attention to strong shoulders.

132

big-night look with pants!

- Dressy, formal pants are sleeker than daytime pants, meaning that they don't have belt-loops or bulky pockets. The fabric should also be a little nicer than what you'd wear during the day, like a soft, lightweight wool, a dressy rayon blend, satin, or even velvet.

- To keep from looking too mannish, wear pants with pointy-toe flats, heels, sandals, slingbacks, or boots. (If you like that boyish look, go ahead and wear your pants with a pair of black lace-up shoes.)

- On top, you can wear a silky white blouse, a fitted button-up vest, a beaded sweater, whatever you'd like. If you wear pants at night, the simpler the colors the dressier it looks, so try wearing all black, or black with white, silver or gold for a more sophisticated, formal look. In the summer, try all white, or dressy white pants with a vivid bright top.

ZOE SALDANA
Crisp white pants like Zoe's were made for dressy summer nights, and when they're paired with black, they really pop. The deep-V neckline is so pretty—a good choice if you're broad on top. And a top that fits low, and hits right at the hips, makes curves on the bottom look slimmer. The bangle bracelets, clutch bag, and dressy sandals are special-event finishing touches.

ELISHA CUTHBERT
Skinny pants that cover most (not all) of your shoes, long beads, and a pale, neutral color scheme can create the illusion of height, making tiny Elisha look long and lean. Because of where her top hits at the hips, it can make bottom-half curves look curvier—which is good if you're straight-up-and-down, and not so good if you're not.

ANNE HATHAWAY
Slim white pants and a slinky top are a chic and sexy alternative for summery nights out. Anne emphasizes her extra-long limbs with this lean look (though her pants may be slightly too long). This look is best for non-dance occasions, because while that strapless top is holding up over her curves now, on the dance floor it might not. Try dark pants if you're curvy on the bottom and obviously, broad shoulders are seriously exposed.

10 TIPS FOR A
FUN, FORMAL NIGHT

Nicole Richie is an expert at dressing for the dance floor.

1 Be you. Even if you try a new style for a big night, make sure you feel comfortable or you'll be second-guessing your choice all night. Don't choose a big fluffy ruffle of a dress if you never even wear skirts to school. You'll feel like you're wearing a costume. Try dressy tuxedo pants and a beaded top instead, or even a dress with a simpler look.

2 Comfort is key. Too-high heels, anything itchy, too tight, or that restricts your movement (and your good time), are bad choices. If you love a dress but it's a little scratchy, find a slip to wear under it that will protect your skin. And always practice wearing your shoes around the house before you wear them to a special event.

TIP: Use a rough nail file or sand paper to scratch up the soles of new shoes before you wear them. This helps prevent slippery accidents on the dance floor—or anywhere else, for that matter!

3 Put your outfit to the stress test. In the fitting room, sit down, bend over, and move around to see how it feels. A strapless dress that slips down, a bodice that's hard to breathe in when you sit, or straps that keep slipping off your shoulder are no-gos. You can even bust a few dance moves (you may feel a little dorky, but you'll be happy when you're comfortable at the dance!).

4 **Shop for vintage gowns.** Thrift stores are great places to find "gently used" evening gowns. Instead of buying the new dress made to look like it's from the 1980s, buy one that was actually made in the '80s for a lot less. It's a guaranteed one-of-a-kind. Consignment shops that resell more current clothes from the last few years are a good place to look for bargains, too.

5 **Sew on a strap, hike up a hem, snip off a bow.** Customize a dress any way you want to make it more comfortable or more "you." Say you found the absolutely perfect dress of your dreams, if it weren't for that cheesy flower stitched on at the waist! Before you put it back on the rack, take a closer look. Most of the time, these little details are tacked on with just a few stitches and can be removed with just a few snips of the scissors. If the annoying part, like a ribbon at the waistband, is covering up a seam and can't be removed, keep looking! If you'd love a strapless dress more if it actually had straps, sewing them on is a cinch.

> **TIP:** You can even use a wide satiny ribbon from the fabric store to create straps. Pin one end of the ribbon, with an inch or two extra length, onto the back of the bodice of the dress where a strap would be. Put on the dress. With help from a friend, pull the ribbon over your shoulder and pin it to the front of the bodice. Make sure it's tight enough to offer some support. Take off the dress, and stitch the ribbon into place.

6 **Don't be afraid of hand-me-downs.** Ask an older sister, cousin, neighbor, or friend who goes to a different school to borrow a special-occasion dress if you can. Chances are, she's worn it only once

and no one will remember seeing her in it. Just make sure it fits! If you have to take it in a little, ask permission first, and then have the seamstress let out the stitches after you've worn it. Spend the money you saved on fun new accessories—big, rhinestone earrings, a bold necklace, even a sequined scarf—and make the look your own.

7 **Dress up separates.** Pair a sequined camisole or crisp white

Katharine Heigl's fur stole adds warmth and bold color to an otherwise neutral outfit, both pieces of which she can wear again and again—separately!

shirt with a full taffeta skirt, or a beaded sweater with a simple skirt. They're more practical because they can be mixed and matched, and worn again and again. After the party's over, you can wear that camisole with jeans and get extra mileage from your money and your clothes.

8 **Wear the right undergarments.** A strapless bra, undies that are smooth enough not to show through a sheer fabric, or a slip that keeps a dress from clinging to your legs with static are essential. No one wants to be fiddling with out-of-control underwear all night. Look for flesh-colored bras and underwear that won't show through your clothes. And, if you need to buy new underthings, bring your dress to the store with you when you try them on to guarantee the perfect fit.

9 **Have long dresses hemmed after you find the right shoes.** If the dress is half an inch too long, you're likely to trip and rip it. Half an inch too short and you'll look like you're wearing a borrowed dress. When a dress fits you just right, it looks like it was custom-made only for you, and it's worth the extra effort.

10 **Find the right bag and coat.** Buy one small evening bag in silver or gold (to match the jewelry you'll wear) and it will go with just about any color or style you wear. It's a good investment that you'll have for years! A simple shawl or a cardigan sweater can be a good alternative to a bulky coat for big nights on the town, when you won't be standing outside much. A fake fur scarf can also be a glamorous way to stay warm at fancy winter parties.

Be an
ALL-STAR

SHOPPER

HAVE SUPERSTAR STYLE WITH LESS THAN STELLAR FUNDS

Want to have great style on a realistic budget? Buy the best essentials you can afford and build from there—this is a situation when less can definitely be more. For example, one pair of jeans that fit you like a glove and go with everything you wear, makes a lot more sense than two or three pairs with a decent fit that you think are just okay. Buy great basics, and add your own style spin with accessories.

A good way to think about a clothes budget is to divide it up according to how often you're going to be wearing each particular kind of clothes. Since you wear school clothes more than going-out weekend clothes, you should spend more on those things. One exception: If you wear a school uniform, then the weekend is the only time you get to relax and wear fun clothes.

When you're breaking down your budget, think of it like this:

SCHOOL CLOTHES = 5 DAYS

What you wear to school should be where the bulk of where your money goes, unless you wear a uniform. (In that case, spend your money on the perfect shoes, earrings, or accessories that can add personal touches to your look.)

WEEKEND/GOING-OUT CLOTHES = 2 DAYS (MAYBE 3, TOPS).

It's tempting to blow your entire budget on sparkly, fancy camisoles, sweaters or silky tops, but be realistic. If you know you can only wear something 3 times a month, what's the point? Buy one or two tops a season, at a discount store or on sale, and you'll be set.

HANGING OUT/BUMMING AROUND CLOTHES = ZERO

Last year's school clothes are this year's bumming-around clothes. Unless you wear a school uniform, don't waste your money on hanging-out clothes (how many pairs of sweatpants does one person need, anyway?).

BUDGET BREAKDOWN:

Every month, spend 20 days at school and 8 nights going out. If you have a budget of $100 per month, your spending should look something like this:

• TWO-THIRDS of your budget should be spent on school clothes: That's about $65.

• ONE-THIRD of your budget should be spent on weekend clothes: That's a little less than $35.

NOTE TO UNIFORM WEARERS: The equation should be ONE-HALF school (buying the right accessories is essential when you can't change up the outfit) and ONE-HALF casual time.

SPEND OR SAVE?

Here are some tips about which items deserve a splurge, and how you can save a little on the rest:

EXPENSIVE FABRICS VS. CHEAP MATERIALS

SPEND on basic pieces in quality fabrics like 100% cotton, wool, cashmere, or silk.

SAVE on rayon camisoles and lightweight dresses.

EVERYDAY BASICS VS. FUN ACCESSORIES

SPEND on quality basics that you'll wear again and again.

SAVE on bold statement pieces that liven up the basic pieces.

Sienna Miller wears the same great-fitting jeans with a ton of different accessories, like Indian sandals, a thrift store jacket, shearling boots, and big black sunglasses.

A black pencil skirt like the one on **Amanda Bynes** is a superb splurge, since you can wear it so many ways on so many days.

NEUTRAL COLORS VS. OUT-THERE BRIGHTS

SPEND on basics in dark colors (like a pair of pants that you can wear twice a week…and nobody notices!).

SAVE on over-the-top brights (like an orange shirt that you can wear once a month…and everybody notices!).

STAND-BY CLASSIC BLACK DRESSES VS. UNFORGETTABLE DRESSES

SPEND on a classic black dress that you can wear 5 different ways with unique accessories.

SAVE by lending a standout dress to a friend (and borrowing one of hers) next time there's a special occasion. That way, you can both get more wear out of that unforgettable dress.

Sophia Bush knows that a straight-across bustline works for her body, whether it's in black or rich navy blue.

Both this black stunner and the statuesque green gown showcase **Venus Williams'** toned shoulders and arms.

HOW TO STRETCH $50

You've got babysitting money, your allowance, or some birthday cash just burning a hole in your pocket, and you want a quick style pick-me-up. Here are three ways to make it last, matched to your style:

BOHEMIAN BANKROLL

$10 Dangly earrings It's the fastest way to change up your look, and the first thing people notice when they talk to you.

Eva Mendes

$10: Skinny scarf Look for one with a metallic thread in it, like gold, and it'll be an instant wardrobe essential, for day and night.

$10: A men's ribbed tank top Don't let anybody give you funny looks when you head to the men's department to buy a long tank top in black, navy, or white (in size extra-small or small) to layer under or over your clothes. They're cheaper here than just about anywhere else.

$5: Vintage skirt You're known for your eclectic taste, so you can get away with a crazy skirt that you picked up in a vintage store.

$15: Thick, patterned tights This is one accessory that's worth the splurge, since cheap, thin tights can pull, snag, sag, and be generally uncomfortable. Buy a solid color with a fun pattern, like herringbone or check, and wear them with short or long skirts and dresses.

SPORTY SPENDER

$30: Colorful hoodie You live in sweatshirts and jeans, so why not step it up a little bit? Find a version of your favorite staple in a bright color and maybe a snug fit for a leaner look. It's your version of dress-up!

$5: Colored shoelaces It's so much less expensive than buying a new pair of shoes, it's ridiculous. Change your laces every week, if you want, for a fast and easy shoe makeover.

$15: Leather cuff bracelet When long beads and rhinestones don't cut it, a simple cuff is all the jewelry you need. Try one in basic brown, black, or an unusual color and rev up your look.

PREPPY PAYOFF

$30: Casual sneakers In our book, you can never have too many low-top Converse. Buy them in blue, black, white, off-white, even red, and wear them with just about anything you own, at school or out on the town.

$15: Snug-fitting polo shirt Check out the boys' department for a good deal. A boys' size 10 is about the equivalent of a size 5, and a 12 is about a 7. It'll be snug in the arms and shoulders and will just graze the waistband of your pants, but in a cute way!

$5: Sweet socks A pair of cute argyle or striped socks can be an instant and easy way to update any look. Wear them with flats, or even open-toed sandals or heels, for a shock of unexpected color and pattern.

HOW TO WORK . . .

. . . THE MALL

PROS

- You get a real handle on trends, since you can see so many stores at once.
- It's easy to put an outfit together by picking up things at various stores.

CONS

- The stores can be really expensive.
- Because everybody else shops there, you could end up looking like a style-clone (not great).

TIP: Go shopping with friends for fun, cheap accessories and the occasional cute top on sale. Shopping for big-ticket items is best done when you have the time to see what fits you the best, as well as the time to concentrate on what you're spending.

. . . THE DISCOUNT STORE

PROS

- They're all marked down so much from the original price, they are affordable!
- These stores carry brands that you won't see at the mall, so you've got a good chance to find something special no one else will have.

CONS

- It can be so exhausting to go through all of that stuff, which is often so disorganized that it's hard to find your size.

TIP: Take a couple of hours to really power through a discount store. Grab things you like when you see them and put them back later if you change your mind. Keep an open mind—you may not find the thing you need, but you may find an unexpected wonder!

. . . THE OUTLET MALL

PROS

- It's got the convenience of a mall—everything is close together—without the high prices.

CONS

- A lot of what they sell are factory rejects or leftovers from stores and are in extreme sizes or damaged.
- "Clearance disease"—the sickness that causes you to buy things you don't like just because they're on sale.
- Usually, all sales are final.

TIP: While the occasional amazing bargain can be found at outlet malls, that's pretty rare. Look for inexpensive accessories from big designers. Examine everything closely for irregularities. Something simple like a missed button can easily be fixed, but a big grease stain can't.

. . . THE VINTAGE STORE

PROS

- They're packed full of one-of-a-kind items that you probably won't find anywhere else.
- Many designers look to the past for ideas, and you can find the original versions of current trends for a whole lot less at a vintage store.

CONS

- The clothes can be dingy and smell musty.
- Some vintage stores are disorganized and sometimes a little dirty.
- The sizes are odd and sometimes it's difficult to find something that will fit.

TIP: Never buy anything that smells terrible (it'll never come out) or needs major repairs (you'll never fix it, and even if you do it may not look right). Vintage shopping requires some patience, but the rewards can be so worth it. Look for party dresses or costume jewelry, which are in great supply here.

THE 10 SECRETS OF SUPER SHOPPERS

1 Bring along a calculator (or use the one on your cell phone) to help you make shopping decisions based on tax, percentage markdowns, etc.

2 Always ask a salesperson about the store's next sale (no one wants to buy a sweater the day before it's marked down). Befriend the sales staff at your favorite stores, or sign up for their mailing list so you can find out about sales before they happen—and never pay full price!

Eva Longoria looks for bargains in NYC.

3 Don't shop when you're hungry. If you're hungry, it clouds your judgment: you're either light-headed from hunger and rushing through the store so you can get to lunch or just plain not feeling good (and therefore not feeling good

about yourself). Bring an emergency snack in your bag if you have to, or schedule your shopping trips for after lunch. If you're having a hard time making a decision about something, ask if you can put it on hold for a couple of hours and come back after you eat.

4 Bring a bottle of water in your bag to stay hydrated. When you're dehydrated, you're tired and sluggish and generally not feeling great. If you're on your feet for hours, it can be exhausting, and you need all the help you can get. You'll never catch a celebrity shopper without a giant bottle of water in her oversized bag, and now you know why.

5 Wear comfortable shoes (if you're planning to shop for shoes, bring the correct weight socks along for the type of shoes you're planning to buy). If you're going to be walking the mall or standing up sifting through racks at a discount or vintage store, it helps to be comfortable. Pinched toes or blisters can cut your trip short and make you miss out on something cute.

6 Keep an open mind. The best bargains are usually found in the off-season—summer clothes are on sale in fall, winter clothes are marked down in spring,

etc. If you leave the house thinking that you need a red T-shirt and a red T-shirt only, you can miss out on a lot. If you're still growing, you might need to pay attention to what may or may not fit six months down the road.

7 Sizing can be really irregular, so ignore the numbers and look for the best fit instead. One store's 5 can be another store's 7, or even a 3. If you're usually a small but a medium fits better, who cares? What's important is that the clothes fit correctly—they don't bind or pinch your skin, or sag and droop. No two girls ever have the exact same body, do they? While it helps to have a general idea of what size you wear, it really isn't as important as how it fits your body.

The one constant in Sienna Miller's wardrobe? A shopping bag.

8 Consider the "price per wear." Remember the equation from the budget section? If you're going to wear something for years until it falls apart, it's worth the investment.

Paris Hilton may be Kitson's best customer.

9 Check for snags, holes, stains, tears, pen marks, or other damage before you buy anything. A missing button can be replaced. But a makeup stain on the collar of a white shirt can be tough to remove, and impossible to return once you've bought it.

10 If you can't wear a new item with at least two things you already own, skip it. You may love that crazy vest you found for 70% off, but if you have to buy an entire outfit to wear with it, it's no bargain.

UNDERSTANDING QUALITY AND VALUE: NO-REGRETS SPLURGES!

FIVE REASONS WHY CLOTHES ARE EXPENSIVE

1 FABRIC Natural fabrics are more expensive than synthetics and usually hold up better. When you're buying everyday pieces, check the fabric content and try not to splurge on an acrylic blend that won't feel so great against your skin. (NOTE: Clothes made of natural fibers may need extra care. Read the label before you buy anything.)

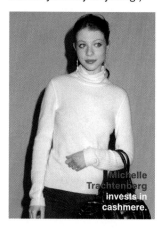

Michelle Trachtenberg invests in cashmere.

2 FIT Which do you think fit better, pants cranked out by the thousands or pants that are sewn a few batches at a time? Splurge on a pair of pants that will last a few years rather than replacing the cheap ones every year.

3 DESIGNER LABELS It's really expensive to wear head-to-toe designer labels. If you must have a piece with a logo, buy something tiny, like a key chain. You get a little bit of the lifestyle without breaking the bank.

Gwen Stefani probably gets a discount on L.A.M.B. stuff.

4 DETAILS Beading, leather trim, and embroidery all make the cost of clothes soar. Before you splurge on an item that has these details, make sure that it's something that will last more than one season.

The beading on Mya's camisole makes it splurge-worthy.

5 STORE MARK-UPS Where do you usually shop? If it's at a store with spotless dressing rooms, soft lighting, and dozens of employees, you're probably paying more. Look at discount stores or shop online for the same merchandise without the overhead.

NO-REGRETS SPLURGE CHECK LIST:

Make sure every splurge fits the following criteria:

• Does it fit perfectly? If not, don't buy it. Having it altered will cost more, and even then there's no guarantee that it will fit well.

• What's its shelf life? Will you still love it next month? Next year? Anything that's super-trendy isn't worth the money. Invest in classic clothes that have a longer shelf life.

• Does it suit your style? A lacy blouse on triple-mark-down at your favorite discount store isn't a bargain if you haven't touched a ruffle since the third grade.

• Is it totally unique or an everyday basic that will last nearly forever, like a perfect party dress that fits you like a glove for just

$15? BUY IT! Even if you don't have an occasion to wear it now, you will! Or the ideal blue cardigan in your size? Even if it's a little more than you want to spend, if it's still affordable, BUY IT! You'll wear it for the next 5 years.

• While you're trying it on, do you want to wear it for 24 hours straight? It's always a good purchase when you never want to take it off.

• If you're hesitating, check the store's return policy before you buy it. If you can't return it for a refund (not just store credit), put it back. If you're still thinking about it a week later, go back. If it's been sold, it wasn't meant to be.

• What's the "price per wear?" Remember that blue cardigan? Let's say it cost you $50. If you wear that cardigan once a week for the next 6 months, that's 24 times, or about $2 per wear. And if you wear it twice a month for the next two years? That's 48 times, or just a little more than $1 per wear. On the other hand, a $15 T-shirt that shrinks so much the first time you wash it costs $15 per wear. Which one do you think is the bargain?

143

9

CLOSET M

AKEOVER

Your best outfit ever may already be in your closet! Streamline your wardrobe and see for yourself.

HOW TO CLEAN YOUR CLOSET

Love it or leave it? It's a tough question to ask, but it may be time to say good-bye to pilly or shrunken sweaters, dingy T-shirts, and those jeans you haven't worn since the 5th grade. Weed through your wardrobe to find what works . . . and what doesn't.

Overstuffed closets take a lot of the fun out of getting dressed. How can you expect to look your best every day when your clothes are dirty, disorganized, wrinkled, or missing-in-action in a messy closet? Balled-up under your bed, stuffed in the corner, or jammed on a hanger: Your clothes won't be good to you unless you're good them. A thorough closet reorganization is the best place to start.

The next rainy Saturday when you're looking for something to do, skip the mall and the movies and practice a little wardrobe management instead. Chances are, there are some great things that you don't even remember you have. And sorting through all of the clothes you own may give you fresh ideas about new outfits.

TIP: This is a big project, and it can be a big mess, so make sure you have enough time to put everything back in order once you pull your closet apart.

Start with your hanging clothes—then move on to your shelves and drawers.

Pull everything out and lay it on your bed or the clean floor.

Go through the things you have, one by one.

FOR EACH ITEM, ASK YOURSELF THE FOLLOWING QUESTIONS:

1. DOES IT FIT?

• Try it on. If it fits, put it in a pile of other things like it (pants with pants, sweaters with sweaters, tops with tops, etc.).

• If it's too big and can be taken in or hemmed, put it in a fix-it pile.

• If it's too small, it's going to charity (or a little sister, a younger cousin, or a neighbor who could use it), or it can be recycled to make a new accessory (check out page 152 for some cool ideas).

2. IS IT DAMAGED?

• If there's a button missing, or a hem that's fallen and needs to be re-sewn, toss it in the fix-it pile.

• For a sweater covered with pills (those annoying little balls of fuzz), you could try using a special machine called a sweater shaver to remove them (or very carefully with a pair of scissors and a LOT of patience).

• If something is damaged beyond repair, get rid of it.

• If it has extreme sentimental value, put it away in a box. Don't let it take up valuable closet space.

3. WHEN WAS THE LAST TIME YOU WORE IT?

• Can't remember the last time you wore it? Can't think of anything you own that goes with it? Not sure if you even LIKE it anymore? It may be time to say good-bye. Toss it in the give-away or recycle pile.

- Not sure? Try this trick: Put it in a box with the other "undecided" items and mark the date on the outside of it. In three months, if you haven't thought about anything in the box, give it away or recycle them. But, if you find yourself digging through the box in search of that special something, that means you really like it and should keep it.

Once you've sorted through everything in your closet, it's time to put the things you're keeping back in a way that make sense to you. First, separate your clothes by season, putting the clothes that are right for the current season in the place where you can get to them easily. Then pick the strategy that works best for you.

- Group clothes according to their function: Match pants with pants, jeans with jeans, short sleeves with short sleeves. This makes finding what you're looking for a snap.

- Try hanging clothes in groups according to color: Browns hang with beige and tan. Baby blue and navy share the same space.

Color- coordinating your closet lets you see what works together, and may give you new ideas about outfits, and how to coordinate the colors in your wardrobe.

- Divide your clothes according to where and when you wear them: One section for school; one for weekends; one for dress-up.

DRAWERS AND SHELVES!

Once your closet is complete, move on to that dresser.

- Weed out the old, never-worn T-shirts and either give them away or recycle them.

- The same goes for undies, socks, sweatshirts, sweatpants, and whatever else you have stuffed in there.

- Then put the keepers back in a neat, organized way: Put long sleeves in the same pile as other long sleeves, jeans with jeans, socks with other socks, etc. Just wait and see! Getting dressed is going to be a whole lot easier this way (and will save you time and frustration).

TIP: Not enough room in your T-shirt drawer? Try rolling them instead of folding them. You'll fit more into the drawer, and they won't wrinkle as much. Fold a T-shirt in half lengthwise, then fold in the sleeves. Roll from the bottom hem up to the neck.

WASH AND WEAR: CARING FOR YOUR CLOTHES

Infrequent cleaning is the secret to keeping all of your clothes longer, even if you just throw them in the washer. Unless you've worked-out or done some incredibly dirty chore in your clothes, they probably aren't that dirty. A T-shirt can get two wearings (as long as it passes the smelly underarm test): once to school and once on the weekend. Jeans can be worn three times between washings.

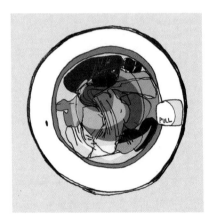

LAUNDRY 101:

- White clothes are washed with other whites in a hot cycle.

- Pastel or bright-colored clothes should be washed together in a warm cycle.

- Darks and denim go together in a cold wash.

- Just about any wash cycle should have a cold rinse, to conserve energy and to prevent fading. Use only the recommended amount of detergent (even less for small loads or anything that's not too dirty).

- If you have to use the dryer, set it to the shortest amount of time possible. Over-heating your tees, jeans, and even your undies can lead to shrinkage. The heat is hard on any elastic or spandex material that gives things their stretch, causing them to lose their shape faster.

- Jeans should be worn more than once between washings (unless you spill something or stain them) to prevent fading and shrinking. Turn your jeans inside out when you wash them. It also keeps the color from fading fast.

- Did you accidentally leave a red sock in the wash and turn everything you own pink? Before you put the clothes in the dryer, try washing them again with a non-chlorine bleach to remove the stains.

DRY-CLEANING 101:

- A dry-clean-only tag on your clothes should come as a warning: The up-keep of this item may be a lot more than you might want to spend. Any dry-cleaned item should be worn at least two, preferably three or more times between trips to the pros. But even at $3.00 per cleaning, a $30 top doubles its cost in the first year you own it. And the chemicals used in the process are hard on the environment (and on your clothes, causing the fibers to wear, fade and fall apart faster).

- There are a few things you can do to keep your clothes fresh between cleanings. Try putting sweaters or wool pants that have absorbed any odors (like food smells) in the dryer on the fluff cycle, with no heat, and a dryer sheet. That will eliminate most bad smells and delay dry-cleaning for another wear. If you spill or stain something, try to remove it with a damp rag and lukewarm water.

- Some light-weight cotton, silk, or wool clothes have a dry-clean or hand-wash option. Try alternating cleanings with hand-washing. It may require a little ironing after it's hung to dry (at a low temperature-setting on the iron, set for the specific fabric type), but it'll save some money and is gentler on your clothes.

- If your clothes are stained, point out and describe the stains to the cleaner. Different cleaning chemicals are used for different stains, and this will help them figure out the best approach to cleaning your clothes.

- Take off dry-cleaning bags immediately after you take your clothes home. This will help your clothes "air out" and not trap the fumes from chemicals (which some people believe are toxic) in your closet.

HAND-WASHING 101:

- Hand-washing your bras, tights and fancy undies is the best way, but there are plenty of girls who still run these items through the washer and dryer cycles. It's up to you, but trust us, they won't last as long. The bra hooks and under wire get caught on other clothes, tights get tangled, yanked, and stretched in the spin cycle, and the elastic on nice undies is stretched out of shape in the washer and dryer, too.

- Washing clothes by hand is easier than it seems. Buy a gentle laundry soap designed for delicates. Fill a bathroom or laundry room sink with water and add a capful of liquid detergent, or a small scoop of powdered laundry soap. Use only warm or cool water, not hot, which can make things shrink and fade.

- Don't overcrowd the sink. Do a couple of sink-fuls of wash if you have to. Put your clothes in the soapy water (lights with other lights, darks with darks) and let them soak for at least 3 minutes. Squeeze the soapy water through your clothes and swish them

around. Let them soak for another few minutes, then rinse them with cool water until it runs clear (there are no bubbles in sight).

- Sweaters should be laid out flat on a towel or a special net sweater-drying rack to maintain their shape. Either pin hand-washed clothes to a clothesline or hang them on a drying rack (in the bathtub or outside on a warm sunny day).

HANGING AND FOLDING 101:

- Clothes that are hung on hangers, folded or stored properly don't wrinkle as much, and therefore don't need to be pressed or cleaned as much. Yet another great reason for keeping your closet organized.

- Pants should be folded in half, so the legs are together, and placed over the bar of a hanger. This prevents most creasing and wrinkling. If space is tight, try folding two pants on one hanger. Hangers with spring-clamps are also designed for pants: Clip the hems of the pants into the clamps and let the waist band hang down to prevent bunching and wrinkling.

- Keep tops on hangers with at least one button buttoned so they keep their shape. Make sure the hook of each hanger is facing in the same

direction so they're easy to pull out and don't get tangled with each other.

- Most sweaters should be folded neatly and put on a shelf, not hung on a hanger in the closet. Hangers can stretch out shoulders and leave bumps on the shoulders, which are hard to get rid of.

IRONING 101:

- Use the iron at the coolest setting possible for the fiber: Cotton and wool need the highest temperature, silk much cooler.

- Always fill the iron with water. Steam helps to press out creases and prevents the iron from burning your clothes.

- For really light and delicate clothes, try putting a pillow case or a small towel between the iron and the clothes to keep the hot metal surface from scorching the fabric.

- Push the iron with small, jiggly movements to work out any creases or wrinkles in the fabric. Let your clothes cool before putting them on.

- If you iron your jeans, remember to turn them inside out. If you don't, the denim can get shiny and lose its color.

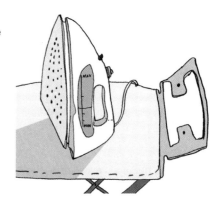

SWAP MEET PARTY

Have a clothes-exchange party with friends.

Who doesn't love to look through their friends' closets? It's always fun to see what they've got stowed away in there. Some of the things they're tired of may be just what you're looking for, and vice versa. Before you cart all of your unwanted clothes away to the Salvation Army, host a swap meet party. It's like a 100% free shopping spree for you and your friends!

Never Been Kissed

HERE'S HOW IT WORKS:

- Pick a Friday or Saturday and invite all of your friends: More people means more great stuff to choose from!

- Ask them to stuff all of the clothes they don't want—old T-shirts, jeans that don't fit, anything (with their parents' permission, of course!)—into bags and bring it over. Moms can even donate stuff from their closets that they don't want anymore, too, just for fun!

- Have plenty of drinks and snacks on hand, because a free-for-all frenzy is about to begin! Order a pizza and make a whole night of it.

- When everyone arrives, dump all of the bags into a big pile in the middle of the floor. If your room isn't big enough, ask if you can take over another space. Put an old, clean sheet down in the garage if you have to. Mix up the clothes in a big jumble.

- Ready, set, SHOP! Check out the goods. Sift through the clothes to see what is close to your size. Feel free to sneak away to try something on if you have to. You'll be surprised to see what's in there!

- Turn it into a funny dress up party. See who can make the weirdest, greatest outfit out of what's in the pile.

- At the end of the night, have people put the stuff they want to take home back in the bag that they brought. It's an instant wardrobe update that didn't cost a thing!

MORE IDEAS:

- Rent movies with great shopping or dress-up scenes, like *Pretty Woman, Never Been Kissed, Pretty in Pink* (a 1980s movie starring Molly Ringwald, whose character makes her own prom dress and has great vintage style), *Clueless,* or *Legally Blonde,* and make a whole fashion event of the night.

- Get crafty and try to revamp some of the old clothes you don't want. Decorate old jeans, or break out the scissors and beads or ribbons and create new T-shirts!

- Have everyone bring a stack of their favorite old magazines and make style diaries together. Tear out pictures of favorite outfits and paste them into the pages of a notebook, making collages of terrific looks, and giving you lots of great dress-up ideas.

Pretty Woman

Clueless

RECYCLE THE REJECTS

All you need are a few D.I.Y. ideas to turn potential trash into new treasures.

TO DYE FOR:

Faded T-shirts, tank tops, skirts and pants get a second wind with dye.

1. STOVETOP DYEING:

• Fill a pot with hot water (don't use one of your mom's favorites—the dye will stain the pot) and mix in the dye.

• Wet the item and add it to the pot.

• Bring the brew to a simmer for at least 30 minutes. Stir it occasionally.

• Turn off heat, remove item from pot, and rinse it under cool water until the water runs clear.

• Wash it with mild detergent and let it air dry or use the dryer.

2. WASHING MACHINE DYEING:

• Mix dye with lukewarm water in a bowl or bucket. Put it aside.

• Toss item into washer and set to PREWASH cycle using the hot/cold water setting.

• When the buzzer goes off at the end of the prewash cycle, pour dye into the detergent receptacle. Let it run.

• When the cycle is finished, let the item air dry or use the dryer.

Don't forget to run the washer with hot water and detergent when you're finished so you don't dye the next load of laundry!

3. TIE DYEING:

• In addition to dye, you'll need rubber bands or string, buckets or pots for each dye-bath you'll be making (from one up to 5 different colors), a long-handled spoon, scissors, and detergent.

• Put on rubber gloves and make all your dye-baths by mixing the dye with very hot water.

• Take the article that you're dyeing and grab a large section of fabric.

• Wrap the rubber band or string at the base of the fabric section. The area under the rubber band is protected from the dye, so think about which parts you want to stay light, and then fasten them off with more rubber bands.

• Starting with the lightest color, dunk the item in dye and leave it for five to ten minutes.

• Rinse the item with cool water after each dye so that colors don't blend in the bowls.

• Add more rubber bands and repeat in your next color, then rinse. Do this until you've used all the dye or you feel happy with the project.

• Remove all of the bands and then rinse in cool water until the water runs clear.

• Wash it with mild detergent and warm water. Gently squeeze out remaining water, and hang to dry.

4. DIP DYEING:

• You'll need the same stuff as above, but use string or wide strips of cloth instead of rubber bands. Put on your gloves and make your dyebaths.

• Wrap sections of the item in the string or strips of cloth. Starting with the lightest color first, dunk the item in the dye and leave it there for between five and ten minutes..

• Rinse the item with cool water after each dye so that colors don't blend in the bowls.

• You can also only use one color: soak a four- or five-inch section to start, then submerge more of it every five minutes. When you're finished it will be lighter on one side and will get gradually darker.

5. DYE YOUR CLOTHES WITH TEA, COFFEE, OR KOOL-AID!

• Brew a few cups of tea—black tea and Red Zinger work best. Soak a light colored T-shirt or tank for a few hours.

• Coffee works well if you're trying to dye something brown.

• You can also use Kool-Aid! Dissolve a packet (the unsweetened kind) in a microwave-safe bowl with a few cups of water. Put white- or cream-colored fabric (nothing with any metal pieces) in the bowl and zap it for two minutes. Leave it for five minutes, then zap it again for two minutes. Rinse the item in slightly warm water and let it air dry.

6. WRITE ON DARK CLOTHES WITH A BLEACH PEN.

A bleach pen removes small stains from white clothes, but the tip can be used just like a marker.

- Put cardboard between the layers of clothing so the bleach doesn't soak through to the other side.
- Write away! Create a design, draw a funny face, whatever you want.
- Toss it in the washing machine (on its own, so the bleach doesn't lighten other dark clothes) and let it air dry or use the dryer.

GET CRAFTY

Experiment with clothes that were on the way to the donation box!

SCISSORS: When it comes to customizing t-shirts, scissors are a girl's best friend.

- Create new necklines! Use shirts that you already have as a guide, if you need to. Or cut V-necks, scoop necks, square shapes, or cut from shoulder seam to shoulder seam for a boat neck.
- Create new sleeve lengths! Long sleeves can become three-quarter length sleeves, short sleeves, cap sleeves, even a tank top.

BADGES: Make a collared shirt look more official by sewing name patches or boy-scout–style badges over your heart.

TRIM: Using a needle and thread, a hot glue gun, or fabric glue, you can transform your cast-offs.

- Decorate the edges, collar, cuffs, or pockets of old shirts with zig-zag

trim, beads, charms, woven trim, chains, even shells. Try sewing mismatched buttons or charms on the front pocket of a T-shirt, or gluing trim along the hem of a sleeve.

- Ribbons and bows can dress up a plain white T-shirt. Sew or glue three different shades of ribbon across the front of your shirt or along the bottom hem.
- A tank top looks super-girly if you gather the fabric at your shoulders with a ribbon and tie it off in a clean knot or a small bow.

IRON-ONS: Make your own iron-ons with your computer using transfer paper, which is now available at most office supply stores.

- Print pictures from your computer onto transfer paper.
- Follow the directions on the back of the transfer paper package. Usually, it just involves cutting out the shape, placing it on the fabric, heating it with an iron, and peeling off the back.
- You can also make transfers using transfer paper in a copy machine at your local copy shop.

PROJECT RUNWAY

Keep your old sweaters, sweatshirts, tees, skirts, and jeans into fun new accessories and decorative pieces that you can long after you've outgrown them by turning them into new accessories and decorative objects.

SWEATERS

Throw 100% wool sweaters into the washer and wash them with hot water, then dry them on high heat. The object is to SHRINK the fibers so that they won't unravel when you cut them (this process is called felting).

* Make a headband! Cut a two- to three-inch strip and sew the ends together so that it fits your head (or just tie it). If it starts to unravel, use yarn in a contrasting color to whip-stitch around the edges (short, diagonal, evenly-spaced stitches over the edges of the fabric).

* You can make patchwork scarves by cutting wider sections and then sewing them end-to-end, making it as long as you want. Same thing here: If it unravels even after you've shrunken the fabric, try whip-stitching the outer edges with yarn in a cute color.

* You can also make pillows with wool sweaters. Cut out two squares and sew three sides of them together. Turn it inside out and stuff it with pillow stuffing from the craft store. Stitch up the third side. You're done!

SWEATSHIRTS AND T-SHIRTS

It's hard to let go of T-shirts and sweatshirts that have sentimental value. Try cutting out the logos or images from the sweatshirts or T-shirts so that you're left with large squares or rectangles of fabric. Have your mom or a friend help you and piece them together so that you are left with a big, comfy blanket that you can cuddle with every day.

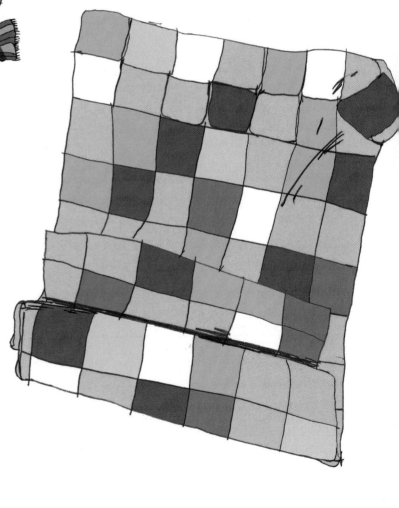

KEEP A STYLE DIARY

After you've cleaned out your closet, swapped with your friends, and gotten all kinds of crafty with your other old stuff, it's a perfect time to start your very own style diary. Stash a notebook in your closet so you can write down ideas when they come to you.

• Have you noticed any obvious "holes" in your wardrobe? Did you have to give away something that didn't fit you any more, but you still loved? Write it down in your style diary under the "Wish List" headline. Next time you're out shopping, bring the list with you so you remember. Or ask for one of the items on your birthday, or for a special holiday.

• Let's say you're getting dressed in the morning, and you think your outfit would be perfect . . . if only you had a wide purple belt! Write it down so you don't forget.

• This is also a great place to store the photos you tear out of your favorite magazines. Next time you're stumped for style inspiration, flip through it for great ideas from your favorite celebrities.

CELEBRITY CLOSETS *Get the inside story.*

KELLY CLARKSON

- Clarkson keeps her T-shirt collection (she has 50!) folded and stacked neatly on shelves in her closet, as well as in her drawers. It's a good way to keep your favorites out on display. When you get tired of one, put it back in the drawer and take a different one out to put back in the rotation.

- She likes to organize her clothes according to the occasion: Bright, flowery cocktail dresses are hung together next to shelves of high-heeled sandals (her favorite for dancing).

- Her two style-splurges are sunglasses and belts, which makes sense for a jeans-loving pop star who lives in sunny Beverly Hills, where dark glasses are an everyday necessity! But she has the right idea: She spends money on accessories that instantly update her look and have a practical function (as in, protecting her eyes keeping her pants from falling down!).

- Clarkson also loves to wear vintage clothes, without ever looking like she's wearing a costume. That's because she mixes the old and the new, '60s bell-bottoms with a new T-shirt, 1940s dresses with up-to-date shoes. That's the trick to making vintage look modern. Mix the old with the new, and don't stick to just one time period, and you'll never look too retro.

HAYLIE DUFF

- She's addicted to jewelry, and not only to expensive pieces—she also favors fun beads in a rainbow of colors and chunky wooden bangles. She keeps her accessories well organized so that even when she's in a rush, the right piece is not hard to find.

- Haylie loves to dress up for events, but on her days off, she prefers low-key cargo pants and jeans paired with cute tank tops, and carries one of her favorite handbags from Chanel or Fendi.

- Not everyone has a closet big enough to fit a seating area and a dresser, but every closet should be a place that's comfortable and feels right to you. Hang up a favorite picture or a poster on the door. Or install hooks so you can display your favorite bags, scarves, and hats as decorations. Make it a pretty, welcoming place so getting dressed everyday is a pleasure.

VANESSA CARLTON

- Carlton's one-of-a-kind style is also very ladylike, so antique screens (that look like they're out of a 1940s dressing room) look right at home with her wardrobe draped over them. If you're in sync with Vanessa's style, next time you're at a flea market, swap meet, or vintage store, look for a folding screen—it feels like you're playing dress up every day!

- Who would have thought that your closet could be a place to decorate and express your style? Carlton's clothes and accessories are so beautiful and decorative, that it's a shame they're hidden away in a closet. Instead of stuffing your costume jewelry in a drawer, display it on stands; or drape a beautiful necklace or scarf over a mirror or bedpost. (Note: For safety's sake, steer clear of lamps).

- Her colorful beaded or sequined shoes are decorative, too, so Carlton leaves them out to dress up her bedroom.

PHOTO CREDITS

20th Century Fox/The Kobal Collection/Suzanne Hanover: 150 t

Access E/wireimage.com: 59 r

Jonathan Alcorn/wireimage.com: 40 l

Vera Anderson: 106 tr; 110 tc

Duffy-Marie Arnoult/wireimage.com: 106 tr; 139 bl

Angela Boatwright/Killer of Giants: 157 b

Jean-Paul Aussenard/wireimage.com: 9 r; 15 br; 25 r; 32 l; 41 l; 42 l; 50 r; 60 tl; 64 l; 74 l; 81 r; 95 bcr; 106 tcr; 118 l; 123 l, r; 124 c; 132 r; 142 r

Tony Barson/wireimage.com: 11 r; 12 r; 54 bl; 60 tc; 128 c

Virgil Bastos/Time Inc. Digital Studio: 71 tc

Ryan Born: 25 l

Alison Buck/wireimage.com: 103 tl

Michael Caulfield/wireimage.com: 39 cl; 58 l; 105 br; 118 cl; 119 cl; 143 tc

Lee Celano/wireimage.com: 65 bcl

Eric Charbonneau/wireimage.com: 30 c; 45 r; 107 c; 112 tl

Djamilla Rosa Cochran/wireimage.com: 19 r; 52 l; 102 tcl; 107 r; 128 r; 132 l; 133 r

Lester Cohen/wireimage.com: 18 r; 30 l; 57 br; 75 r; 95 r; 100 far r; 101 tcl; 105 bl; 109 tl; 131 r

Steve Cohen/wireimage.com: 90–91 all; 94 cl; 95 tcr, cr

Jemal Countess/wireimage.com: 14 r; 31 l; 43 l; 57 bl; 60 tr; 64 r; 102 br; 132 c; 143 bc

Alan Davidson/wireimage.com: 54 tr

Gregg DeGuire/wireimage.com: 8; 13 l; 16 c, r; 17 c; 21 tr; 24 tl; 27 l; 46 r; 58 r; 60 br; 63 tl, bl, r; 98 l; 100 tcl; 108 tl, br; 117 r; 119 cr; 122 l; 126 l; 130 r; 139 tl

James Devaney/wireimage.com: 3 cr; 11 tl; 14 l; 15 tc; 51; 64 bc; 84 l; 94 r; 102 bl; 105 tl; 106 bcr; 110 l; 124 r; 129 r; 131 l, c; 142 l

Jon Furniss/wireimage.com: 39 r; 74 r; 110 bc; 125 c

Ron Galella/wireimage.com: 106 br

Joe Giblin/wireimage.com: 105 tcr

Steve Granitz/wireimage.com: 2 cl; 11 bl; 12 l; 13 r; 15 l; 17 r; 23 r; 41 r; 42 r; 44 l; 54 tl; 55 br; 58 c; 59 l; 62 tr, br; 65 bl; 82 c; 95 bcl; 100 r; 105 tcl; 109 tcr, r; 113 tc; 117 l; 120 cl; 121 cl, r; 122 cr; 124 l; 127 c; 129 l, c; 130 l, c; 131 c

Jesse Grant/wireimage.com: 20 r

Amy Graves/wireimage.com: 68; 99; 125 r

Tom Grizzle/wireimage.com: 107 l

Steve Jennings/wireimage.com: 102 bcl

Dimitrios Kambouris/wireimage.com: 3 r; 10 c; 12 cr; 18 c; 22 tr; 27 r; 31 r; 34 r; 35 r; 39 l; 47 l; 54 br; 64 cl; 72 tr; 75 tl; 105 bcr; 108 bl; 112 bcl, tr, br; 118 cr; 119 l; 121 l; 125 l; 133 l; 139 br

Barry King/wireimage.com: 22 br; 52 r; 94 l; 123 cl; 143 l

Paramount/The Kobal Collection: 151

Jean Baptiste Lacroix/wireimage.com: 20 c

Stephen Lovekin/wireimage.com: 18 l

Jeaneen Lund: 157 t

Dan MacMedan/wireimage.com: 17 l

Time Inc. Home Entertainment

Time Inc. Home Entertainment

Publisher: Richard Fraiman
Executive Director, Marketing Services: Carol Pittard
Director, Retail & Special Sales: Tom Mifsud
Marketing Director, Branded Businesses: Swati Rao
Director, New Product Development: Peter Harper
Financial Director: Steven Sandonato
Assistant General Counsel: Dasha Smith Dwin
Prepress Manager: Emily Rabin
Book Production Manager: Suzanne Janso
Associate Prepress Manager: Anne-Michelle Gallero
Associate Marketing Manager: Alexandra Bliss

Special thanks: Bozena Bannett, Glenn Buonocore, Robert Marasco, Brooke McGuire, Jonathan Polsky, Chavaughn Raines, Ilene Schreider, Adriana Tierno, Britney Williams

© Copyright 2006
Time Inc. Home Entertainment

Published by Teen People Books
Time Inc.
1271 Avenue of the Americas
New York, New York 10020

ISBN 13: 978-1-933405-35-3
ISBN 10: 1-933405-35-X

Teen People Books is a trademark of Time Inc.

We welcome your comments and suggestions about Teen People Books. Please write to us at:
Teen People Books
Attention: Book Editors
PO Box 11016
Des Moines, IA 50336-1016

If you would like to order any of our hardcover Collector's Edition books, please call us at 1-800-327-6388 (Monday through Friday, 7:00 a.m.- 8:00 p.m. or Saturday, 7:00 a.m.- 6:00 p.m. Central Time).

For *Teen People*

Managing Editor: Lori Majewski
Creative Director: Jill Armus
Fashion Director: Jorge Ramon
Photography Director: Doris Brautigan

For Downtown Bookworks Inc.

President: Julie Merberg
Director: Patty Brown
Editor: Sara Newberry
Designer: Elizabeth Van Itallie
Product photography: Anthony Verde & Steve Cohen
Illustrations: Patrick Morgan

Special thanks: Sarah Parvis, Caroline Bronston, Emily Simon